Michael Wordte

South Africa: the Press and the Politics of Liberation

by Chenhamo C. Chimutengwende

Contents

This book is dedicated
to my parents

C.C. Chimutengwende

First published in 1978 by
Barbican Books,
Carlton House, 66-69 Great Queen Street, London EC2B 5BW

SBN 0 905507 00 2 hardback
SBN 0 905507 05 3 paperback

Typeset by Jetset, London WC2 and
printed by Headley Brothers Ltd, Ashford, Kent.

AUTHOR'S NOTE

There are many people whose outstanding helpfulness and support made it possible for me to complete this work. Although it may not be necessary or possible to individually and publicly thank all of them here, I will always remain deeply grateful to them for their help, understanding and commitment which turned out to be indispensable.

This book was originally writen as a dissertation and presented for the MA degree at Bradford University, 1974-75, under the title "Mass Media of Communication in the Perspective of Political Change in South Africa". I must acknowledge my great indebtedness to Professor Adam Curle, Mr Tom Woodhouse and other staff members of the School of Peace Studies, under whose devoted and kind supervision the research was carried out. Without them this study would most probably never have been started.

For much encouragement, suggestions and valuable criticisms I must also thank Dr Job Wabira, Mr Rakhetla Tsehlana, Mr David Sibeko, Dr A. Picho-Owiny, Mr Lewis Nkosi, Dr Wellington Nyangoni, Dr Aaron Mutiti, Mr Dan Mokonyane, Mr Godwin Matatu and Dr John Downing. Their intellectual, political and informational contributions to my research made my task easier than it would have been.

It is important, however, to add that the views, conclusions and mode of expression in this book are entirely my own responsibility. The analysis and political approach in this study do not necessarily reflect the individual views of the people acknowledged.

C.C. Chimutengwende
Bradford University
September 1977

FOREWORD

In the last five.hundred years there have been three great 'communication revolutions'. The first involved the mass production of technology, the second — the Industrial Revolution — resulted in the mass production of writing; the third 'communication revolution' placed significant pressure on scholars to analyse adequately the correlation of the Press and politics.

It is within the purview of communication researchers to explore the political implications of the process of dissemination of information; this is the course pursued here by the author.

His is the first comprehensive work of its kind on the subject. He writes with knowledge of the intricacies of the Press, and is fully qualified to assess its impact and effect on the politics of liberation in South Africa. Chimutengwende unravels the role of the Press very clearly. This book should be a lasting contribution to the literature of communication and political science.

Unlike Wilcox's *The Press in Africa* or Doob's *Communication in Africa* this book is a vigorous study of the machinations of the Press in a specific nation beset with social upheaval. It will close the gap in research on African politics and communication existing since Fanon's *The Wretched of the Earth*. What Fanon did in his treatment of colonial bureaucracy, Chimutengwende accomplishes equally thoroughly within the context of the politics of liberation.

His arguments are coherent and powerful; his style direct and vigorous. The book challenges the accepted concepts of freedom of the press, political liberation, the nature of national internal contradictions, and human rights. The author extends contemporary communication theory into new fields of research. He is not content with mere explanations, but chooses, rather, to make judgements regarding the nature of communication in an oppressive social system. The analysis clearly demonstrates a communicationist's principal task, and Chimutengwende accomplishes it *par excellence.*

To read this book is to learn what is or is not possible in the relationship between the Press and liberation politics. Moreover, it provides a contemporary record and valuable analysis of the struggles in apartheid South Africa.

This book should be read by all concerned with the question of information dissemination in oppressive societies, with racist propaganda, and with communications and political change in South Africa.

Molefi Kete Asante, LHD, PhD,
Professor and Chairperson,
Department of Communication,
State University of New York,
Buffalo, New York 14260,
USA.

Introduction

This book is about the mass media of communication, information work and the politics of liberation in South Africa. The term "press" is often used in this book to cover the whole field of information media in the same way as the designations "press conference" and "freedom of the press" include all the other media of communication. But because of their longer history and level of accessibility to the forces of change in South Africa, this study deals more with the printed than with the broadcast media. Much of the analysis in this study applies to South West Africa and Rhodesia, the two countries which in many ways are an extension of the political and economic system of South Africa.

Every modern state like South Africa has and needs modern communication media. This usually means mass media, ie public television, radio and the large-circulation newspapers; otherwise, the definition may encompass the whole system within which communication on a mass scale takes place in a state and internationally. As instruments or institutions through which society communicates, the mass media are directed towards large audiences and the content is public. This involves the use of technology geared to mass production. Mass communication media cannot operate without considerable capital resources and formal organisation.

Although television, radio and the newspapers play many

common roles, they may not replace each other because each has some functions specific to itself. Being a regular newspaper reader does not prevent one from regularly watching television, listening to the radio and going to the cinema. The choice depends on where one is, what one is able to afford financially or in time, and one's occupation or individual interests. Each medium may represent a different aim and therefore is likely to carry a different analysis or have a different way of presenting news, opinion and analysis. So if one has the time or the money, one will want to use as many of the media as possible for information and entertainment. As Denis McQuail says, "Media use is overlapping, and the more the exposure to one communication source, the higher the probable exposure to others."(1)

The mass media of communication are so immeasurably important that the state, for instance, tries to help the newspapers survive by reducing postage charges for them, subsidising newsprint or even taking them over. Such is their power that whenever a coup d'etat takes place in a country, the mass media headquarters are usually, after the presidential or royal palace, the second area to be captured — in particular the radio and television stations. The reason is that the mass media provide a crucial and direct link between the politicians and the general population.

In this book it is argued that, even if all other factors were conducive to the direct use of the media as tools of political change, the media's role would still be limited by the fact that they tend to reinforce existing beliefs rather than change them and that, where people are influenced to change, the influence is usually indirect. Inter-personal communication is seen as more effective than mass communication. Indeed, the mass media feed inter-personal channels of communication. Each form is therefore complementary to the other. In short, the media are important but not decisive in influencing people.

The media are an integral part of society, a product of the development of society: without society they would not exist independently. As Stuart Hood succinctly puts it, "a fundamental change in the control and organisation of the mass media is impossible without a comparable change in the control and organisation of the societies they serve."(2) Peter Golding elaborates: "The media are involved in the social system. . . They are information brokers, conveying messages in and through social processes . . . they are legitimators of values and institutions in the public arena, conferring status and validity, and setting the agenda for political and cultural debate."(3) The media working as a socialising agent are related to other socialising agencies like the family, school, work and the network of acquaintances.

In South Africa, as in other states, the mass media are social institutions whose role, like that of other institutions, is defined or regulated by the economic and social organisation of society. The problems of the mass media, as these observations have indicated and as will be illustrated later, are therefore a reflection of the socio-economic set-up of a country, ie the distribution of wealth, the level of the conflict between competing social classes and groups, the level of state violence and repression on the one hand and of civilian resistance on the other.

In discussing the role of the media in society, the question "what have been their effects?" usually dominates in South Africa and other capitalist countries. As Melvin L. DeFleur puts it, "The all-consuming question that has dominated research and the development of contemporary theory in the study of the mass media can be summed up in simple terms— namely, 'what has been their effect?' That is, how have the media influenced us as individuals in terms of persuading us to believe in new ideologies, to vote for a particular party, to purchase more goods, to alter or abandon our cultural tastes, to reduce or strengthen our prejudices. . ."(4)

DeFleur's statement identifies the aspects which most mass communications researchers in the West have tended to concentrate on. If some research into other areas like media economics, content and audiences has been undertaken, the idea has been eventually to find out what effects the media have had in a given situation or period. The danger is always present of analysing the effects or work of the media in isolation from the mediating influences and factors or other facets of human society which determine the limitations and possibilities of the mass media in the socio-political process.

The factors which determine the role of the mass media, or how far they can be used as instruments for oppression or liberation are: the nature of the socio-economic system within which the media must operate; the government legislation (which affects the mass media) and its implementation; the actual power of mass communications in general and how human beings are changed or influenced as individuals or as a mass or a community. This study will therefore attempt to cover these factors, especially the first two, which are usually ignored or underestimated, and then briefly summarise the theories of mass communication in terms of the influence and power of the media.

The book aims at examining and analysing the following questions: (a) Why are the information media, especially the press, such a sensitive area in politics? (b) In what ways do the media serve as a leading barometer of the nature and levels of contradictions within the dominant centres of power in the South African ruling class? (c) To what extent can the media be used as an instrument for liberation or for preserving the status quo in South Africa?

The book argues that the question is not simply one of whether the media can be used as an instrument for liberation or oppression. It explains how the media can be used for both, and that in the present circumstances they are used more directly for the forces of oppression than for those of liberation; but it emphasises that, while their indirect use in support of the liberation process remains minimal at this stage, it is, nevertheless, not insignificant.

Many writers on the subject have either dismissed the role of the South African press in the struggle for political change or have vigorously defended it, arguing that the English newspapers in particular are doing their best to expose bravely the racist policies of the government. They fail to discuss the ways by which liberationists disseminate their information and exhortations in South Africa. They fail to discuss the fact that when the media inform different sections of the ruling class about the strengths and weaknesses of and dangers to the system, the oppressed also get informed and plan their strategy and tactics accordingly. The media are expected by the state to support the system as one of its socialisation agencies. They are not above the law, the politics, the economics and the pressures of the state. But supporting the system has its own functional and dysfunctional effects,(5) and from a liberationalist point of view, the latter aspect is extremely important. South Africa is one of the countries which pride themselves on the importance of having a "free" press and media unrestricted by state ownership. The constitution of the Republic of South Africa itself guarantees press freedom. The country's press freedom is often praised by western journalists in Europe and North America. In an editorial comment on press freedom in the Third World, *The Times* (5.8.76) had this to remark: "Where does the standard of freedom fly still without question? In Asia, Japan; in the Middle East, Israel and Lebanon: in Africa only South Africa would pass the test and there with limitations; in Latin America, none . . ." At the International Press Institute conference in Zurich in May 1975, Frank Barton, a former senior journalist in Zambia, being defensive about South Africa, said: "There is more press freedom in South Africa than in the rest of Africa put together." (6) But the question is, freedom under what socio-economic system and to communicate what and for whose benefit or in support, or opposition, to what socio-economic set-up? As Ralph Miliband argues, even in "open societies of advanced capitalism", the mass media are independent only from direct state dictatorship and control, but not free from legal and other official restraints and pressures, nor from the ideology of the main centres of power. Their overwhelming bias is always towards the "bourgeois concensus" when fundamental issues of the present society are involved.(7)

In fact, from 1927 to 1977 South Africa has enacted more than 75 laws which, more and more restrictively, govern the policies and role of the information media.(8) A large number of communicators have been expelled from the country or banned or imprisoned for disseminating information considered by the state to be useful to the internal and external opposition. Even those media which openly support the status quo in South Africa have had to be extremely careful about how to support it without, unintentionally, breaking the law. The South African authorities argue that a state at war against internal and external forces cannot afford an "irresponsible" press. What is "irresponsible" is that which is against the present political and economic set-up of the country as defined by the government. South Africa is a capitalist state which practises bourgeois parliamentary democracy for the ruling white community and extreme racist dictatorship for the indigenous black majority of its population who have no political rights.

In conclusion the book argues that a country whose ideological foundation is threatened by powerful and ever-growing internal and external forces — a country whose socio-economic system is actively opposed by the majority of its people — will not countenance, let alone develop the western bourgeois concept of the "freedom of the press". The more threatened a social system is, the more desperately repressive, arbitrary and voilent it becomes. The increasing and continuous persecution of communicators and the suppression of opposition papers, journalists and other media is taken in the book as one other important sign of the growing strength of the liberationist forces.

The position taken in this book on the role of the press in society corresponds to that of the Colloquium Division of the Second World Black and African Festival of Arts and Culture (FESTAC) in January/February 1977, held in Lagos, Nigeria.

The Report and Recommendations of the Working Group of international media specialists and practitioners dealing with the sub-theme "Black Civilization and Mass Media", compiled by the author for the Group and adopted by the Plenary Session of the Colloquium Division, are included in the appendices of this book.

In the appendices are included also the official statements of the main liberation movements of South Africa, which show their views of the past, present and future course of the liberation struggle.

As this book was going to press, important developments took place inside South Africa which provoked serious international reactions and no doubt contribute to the intensification of the campaign to ostracise the apartheid regime of South Africa. Liberationist groups, many of which are dealt with in Chapter Three of this book, and two newspapers with a wide circulation among Africans were prescribed by the South African government on October 19, 1977. As the Postscript to this book shows, these developments confirm the basic conclusions of the present study.

Notes and References

1. McQuail, Denis: *Towards a Sociology of Mass Communications*, Collier-McMillan, London, 1972.
2. Hood, Stuart: *The Mass Media*, Macmillan, London, 1972, page 93.
3. Golding, Peter: *The Mass Media*, Longman, London, 1974, pages 78 and 102.
4. DeFleur, Melvin L.: *Theories of Mass Communications*, David McKay Inc., New York, 1973, page 118.
5. Wright, Charles R.: *Mass Communication*, Random House, New York, 1959, pages 16-18.
6. See *Sunday Telegraph*, London, May 18, 1975.
7. Miliband, Ralph: *The State in Capitalist Society*, Quartet Books, London, 1973, pages 196-7.
8. See *The Guardian*, London, March 14, and 16, 1977.

Chapter 1:

The Press and the Socio-economic System

The level of development and sophistication of the press in a
given society clearly reflects the level of development and
sophistication of that society. The press does not exist in a
vacuum, but is a social institution established by society to
perform particular functions, and society maintains its
institutions only when they carry out their designated
functions. The development of the press is an integral part
of the development of a nation, and the development of a
nation necessarily includes the development of its press as
one of its social institutions.

The dominant political ideas at any given stage in the history
of a country must be reflected in or supported by the national
institutions and centres of power — otherwise those ideas
cease to be dominant: while there is no such thing as absolute
peace among the various institutions or organs of the state,
there must nevertheless be some equilibrium among them —
sufficient to permit the maintenance of the status quo.

If a country is fascist or liberal or capitalist or socialist or
Christian, the press, as one of the major institutions through
which that system communicates, must support that set-up,
to some extent at least, or else a disastrous conflict will ensue.
By whatever means, there must be the necessary degree of
congruency. The state or system, for its maintenance, depends
on the support of its major establishments, which are integral
parts of that system. Some contradictions will always exist,

but as long as a system survives its existence proves that the contradictions have not developed to an explosion point. However, in everything positive there is something negative. It is merely a question of which element is dominant at a given period within the life-span of a system.

The press, whether it is owned by the state, by individuals or groups of people, reflects competing interests within the system. The most represented interests in the press are those of the dominant centres of power in the country. The work, views and plans of the most powerful centres of power dominate the news-content of the press. The reason why there are so many newspapers, magazines, radio systems and other information media is that within the ruling class there are groups with different and competing interests. These groups need the media through which they can express their views and campaign for their causes and in which advertising on their behalf can be carried. In the process, the system unintentionally lays itself bare because of the public nature of its mass communication media.

In order to make a reasonably full use of the information media, a high rate of literacy is necessary, and South Africa as a modern industrialised country has a high degree of literacy. Although the state spends more of its resources on the education of the white ruling minority than on the black majority, literacy among the black people of South Africa is more widespread (in proportion to population size) than in most other parts of the African continent.

South Africa is an industrially developed state, rich and with enormous potential, and alone produces two-thirds of the western world's gold. It has in great quantity most of the minerals essential for heavy industry. The gross value of its agricultural output was R58 million in 1911-12 and by 1964-5 had increased to R980 million. Within a relatively short period South Africa has developed from an ox-wagon transport system with poor communications to be one of the major industrial countries with a road network comparable to that of the USA. It established the necessary infrastructure for a highly developed and well diversified economy, with manufacturing industry now the largest contributor to the national income.

Without a developed modern industry, it is not possible to have modern printing machines and other equipment geared to the mass production of newspapers. Without good roads and a modern transport system, printed material cannot be distributed fully and at once. Without advanced technology, the manufacture of radio and television sets, and the very establishment of radio and television services, is impossible. Without a high level of literacy, the mass communication media cannot be as useful as they are today as instruments of communication between the rulers and the ruled, among the rulers themselves and among the ruled themselves.

South Africa is ruled as an inflexibly militant racist and capitalist state. Its ruling class is defined largely by the colour of its citizens. It is a white settler minority of European origin which uses racism as a philosophy for justifying a rigid capitalist system in which the ruling class is restricted to white people. But this white ruling class has two centres of power, namely the Afrikaners and the English-speaking people. The third element in the situation — outside the power structure — are the black people who have no political rights. In order to identify and understand the major conflicts in South Africa, it would be useful to place them in their historical perspective, showing how the conflicts were created developed and maintained, and how the whole situation is reflected in the organisation, pattern of ownership and control of the press. Without a clear understanding of these conflicts and their development, it would not be possible to fully understand the position of the media in South Africa.

The Republic of South Africa, stretching over 471, 445 square miles, has an estimated population of 22,989,000 people (1974), 3,960,000 of whom are whites. In size of population, therefore, South Africa ranks fourth in Africa, after Nigeria, Egypt and Ethiopia. The first Europeans to settle in South Africa arrived in the seventeenth century. After the Dutch East India Company had established Cape Station in 1652 to provide supplies for the company's trading ships sailing to and from Europe, Dutch farmers (Boers) in the eighteenth century came to settle in the area controlled by the company around the Cape. They took land from the indigenous San and Khoi-Khoi peoples. There were charges and counter-charges of cattle thieving between the whites and the people native to the area. Writing about the indigenous population whom they found in the Cape, Van Riebeck, leader of the first settlers, said in his diary: "If their cattle cannot be obtained in a friendly way why then suffer their thefts without making reprisals which would only be required once, for with 150 men, 10,000 to 12,000 cattle could be secured, and without danger, as many of these savages could be caught without a blow for transmission as slaves to India, as they always come to us unarmed. . ."(1)

In May 1659 war was declared on the Khoi-Khoi and it was not until April 1660 that the Khoi-Khoi were defeated and Van Riebeck informed them that the victorious whites now owned the land. For the Dutch settlers the question of natives was simple: "the natives were just natives; dull, stupid, lazy and stinking." (2) The only distinction between them and wild animals was that the natives could be useful as slaves. With increasing numbers of settlers and slaves, the Cape grew from a mere refreshment station to a colony and, as the colony developed, its population increased and its frontiers expanded. Territorial expansion into the interior brought more wars over land with the Bushmen, Hottentots and the "Bantu" whom the Dutch also called "Kaffirs".

Meanwhile the British were beginning to realise the importance of the Cape Colony as a half-way house between Europe and India; the British empire was also expanding and therefore would need such a strategic colony. In 1806 the British succeeded in taking over the Cape, whose European population was mainly Dutch. In 1820, with a severe unemployment

19

situation in Britain, the government brought 5,000 people to the Cape. (3)

Cecil Rhodes clearly echoed the views of many leading British politicians when he commented on the question of British economic problems to a journalist friend in 1895: (4) "I was in the East End of London (working class quarter) yesterday and attended a meeting of the unemployed. I listened to the wild speeches, which were just a cry for 'bread, bread!' and on my way home I pondered over the scene and I became more than ever convinced of the importance of imperialism. . . My cherished idea is a solution for the social problem, ie, in order to save the 40,000,000 inhabitants of the United Kingdom from a bloody civil war, we colonial statesmen must acquire new lands to settle the surplus population, to provide new markets for the goods produced in the factories and mines. The empire, as I have always said, is a bread and butter question. If you want to avoid civil war, you must become imperialists." Rhodes, who became the Cape prime minister - and a multi-millionaire through Kimberley diamonds - gained control of the area between the Limpopo and the Zambezi rivers, now called Southern Rhodesia (Zimbabwe) by 1893. Rhodes' dream was to extend the British empire from the Cape to Cairo.

The introduction of thousands of British colonists into a community largely of Dutch-speaking people increased Dutch hostility towards the British. Not only did the Boers fear that they would be culturally overwhelmed and destroyed, but also the new English-speaking rulers were passing legislation which restricted their freedom. The colony of the Cape of Good Hope, as it was called in 1834, covered 120,000 square miles and boasted 150,000 people: 65,000 were Europeans, 39,000 slaves, and the rest were supposed to be free indigenous people.(5)

As the Dutch/English conflict escalated, and the Dutch craved more land and freedom from the English-speakers, the Boers moved in groups of families ("Voortrekkers") away from the Cape. One major source of conflict between the

British administration and the Dutch settlers was the administration's "soft" attitude to the non-whites, especially the Emancipation Bill. (6) Piet Retief, leader of one group of voortrekkers, wrote in his manifesto: "We are resolved. . . that we will uphold the just principles of liberty; but whilst we will take care that no one shall be held in a state of slavery; it is our determination to maintain such regulations as may suppress crime and preserve proper relations between master and servant." (7) Since the Africans were not recognised as normal human beings, the "just principles of liberty" were to apply to them only as servants of the white people.

These groups of voortrekkers from the Cape Colony established the Republics of Orange Free State and the Transvaal in the 1830s following wars with the Africans whose land was being wrested from them by conquest. To distinguish themselves from the newly arrived Dutch and those who preferred to speak "High Dutch," the voortrekkers called themselves "Afrikaners" and their language "Afrikaans". The latter largely originates from seventeenth-century Dutch, German, Flemish and Malay dialects. Afrikaans developed into a separate and written language, particularly after the Anglo-Boer War, because of the nationalism of the people of Dutch descent and the need they felt for a separate identity. The latter-day Afrikaans also included words from African languages. By 1925, High Dutch was replaced as one of the official languages of the country by Afrikaans, although some wished to retain Dutch as their main language. Since 1905 there has been a considerable body of literature produced in Afrikaans, some of which are regarded as classics.(8)

The new Boer republics had disagreements with Britain over their boundaries. Gold was discovered at Bethal and then at Lydenburg in 1872; the world's richest diamond field found at Kimberley in 1871 and the world's richest gold deposits located at Witwatersrand in 1886 made a few people extremely rich, while the lot of the majority did not improve. Among the whites there was a struggle for the control of non-white labour. By 1895 more than 70 per cent of the Transvaal's white population comprised people from different parts of the world who had been attracted by the gold fields; most of them were British.

Paul Kruger's government in the Transvaal, or the South African Republic as it was by then called, denied citizenship rights to the foreigners for fear that political power would pass into the hands of the British, who would have been an electoral majority. For some time Rhodes tried to incite the foreigners to rebel against the Kruger regime, until the British government declared war against the Transvaal on October 11th 1899; the Boer Republics surrendered in early 1902 and became British colonies by conquest. During this period the man who framed and enforced British policy was Lord Milner, High Commisioner for South Africa and Governor of the Transvaal and the Orange River Colony; the British Colonial Secretary was Joseph Chamberlain, who was replaced in October 1903 by Alfred Lyttleton. Both colonial Secretaries supported Milner's ideas (9) on South Africa. Lord Milner, who, like Cecil Rhodes, described himself as "an Imperialist out and out", believed that "the racial bond . . . is fundamental; deeper, stronger, more primordial than . . . material ties is the tie of common language, common history and traditions." (9) He believed in the hierarchy of races, with the British permanently at the apex, followed by white people of non-British stock, and then well governed non-whites. The contradictions between British capitalism and the Boer fundamentalist feudal way of life culminated in a .decisive victory for the British. At the same time, the seizure of African lands through violence, treachery and hypocrisy led to the Africans being locked within the forces of production as wage slaves. Finding African cheap labour for the mines involved the intensification of the process of dispossessing the indigenous peoples from their lands. Other methods used for driving Africans into the mines were the poll tax, dog tax and hut tax. Those who could not pay had to seek employment in the mines.

The Boers and the British did not differ on the principle that

Africans should remain second-class citizens of the country, but diverged on methods and style. The Boers were more crude and extreme than the British. The defeated Boers during the negotiations for a peace treaty on 28th February 1901 at Middelburg had told the British that they were opposed to the natives being given the vote in the new colony of South Africa and that the Boers would want a "representative" government. Chamberlain, Milner and Kitchener, the British Commander-in-Chief, accepted the Boers' proposal on native suffrage; the terms offered by the British on 7th March 1901 included the following: "As regards the extension of the franchise to Kaffirs in the Transvaal and Orange River Colonies, it is not the intention of H.M. Government to give such franchise before representative government is granted to those colonies, and if then given, it will be so limited as to secure the just predominance of the white race." (10) Or March 31st 1902, the Boers and the British signed the Treaty of Vereeniging, which included a clause promising equal rights for all white people and self-government as soon as possible; and undertaking not to give Africans the right to vote and that a decision on the issue would be left to the future white independent colonial government. (11) However, the conflict between the Afrikaners and the British continued later at a constitutional and political level.

As a result of the Boers' defeat in the Anglo-Boer war, Transvaal, Orange Free State, Natal and the Cape were brought together by the Constitution of 1909 as the Union of South Africa. Under the leadership of prime ministers Botha, Hertzog, Smuts, Malan, Strydom and Verwoerd, the Union moved further towards independence within the Commonwealth, until 1961 when it became a republic outside the Commonwealth. The interests of the Afrikaners are represented by the National Party, which was reconstituted in 1951 as a merger of the National Party, led by Dr Malan, and the Afrikaner Party. The latter was the smaller, but with a militant and exclusive membership, while the former was a more moderate party with broad South African white

23

nationalist ideals. The two organisations had concluded an election pact after the Malan-Havenga negotiations of 1947. As a prelude to the election pact, Malan had made an approach to the Afrikaner Party in 1943 for Afrikaner unity, which was a popular move.(1 2) The name National Party was retained because "that formerly described the political home of both our cooperting parties, and also included all nationally minded people fom both white language groups . . . Afrikanerdom has risen out of the condition of disunity, impotence and mortification in which it found itself . . . regained its self-respect, and has reached a climax of unity and power.(1 3)

The National Party came to power in 1948 on a programme of apartheid under the leadership of Dr Daniel Malan. Dr Hendrik Verwoerd, Minister of Native Affairs, was one of the chief theoreticians of the policy of apartheid, and became prime minister in 1958 when Strydom, who had succeeded Malan, died. Verwoerd believed that "Apartheid was the least of the three evils — a mixed society, abandoning South Africa, or keeping the Africans segregated . . . he alone had a solution —'baaskap' (white supremacy) and an Afrikaner republic, with a president responsible only to God."(1 4)

The National Party is greatly influenced, as indeed is the whole Afrikaner community's political leadership, by a secret society exclusive to important Afrikaners — the Broederbond. Formed in 1919, it has 11,000 members comprising 500 cells in South Africa who meet in secret and have a secret sign.

All the National Party prime ministers and most of the influential cabinet ministers have belonged to it. Members of its leadership are known as The Twelve Apostles. Its chairman in 1973 was the influential Dr Andries Treurnicht, who is a contender for the premiership of the Republic. Another contender is Dr Connie Mulder, Minister of Information, who is also in the Broederbond. The top Broeders are Professor Gerrit Viljoen, Rector of the Rand Afrikaans University; Professor E.J. Marais, Rector of Port Elizabeth University; E.D. Conradie, Cape Province National Party leader; Rev. D. Benkes, Chairman of the Federazie van

24

Afrikaanse Kultuurvereenigings; Jan Standler, former Deputy Director of Education in Natal; Professor A.N. Pelzer, Registrar of the University of Pretoria; J.J. Strauss, Professor of Political Philosophy at the University of the Orange Free State; and J.M. Faure, Deputy Director of Education in Orange Free State. The Prime Minister, J.B.Vorster, most of his ministers, and Anton Rupert, an internationally prominent business tycoon, are also members of this elite, Vorster himself was interned in the World War II for his Nazi sympathies. Supporters of the Hersigte Nationale Party (see page 30) are also to be found in its ranks, the Broederbond being purportedly above Afrikaner party-politics, and its members forbidden to use it for sectional political advantage. The purpose of this fascist secret society is to promote the political power of Afrikaners in South Africa. It is more than a pressure group, since most of the important government officials belong to it. Indeed it is the mainstay of successive governments of the National Party. But the power of the Broederbond becomes less and less as the Afrikaner power gets more and more threatened and its leadership gets more divided than ever before on what to do.

Apartheid

It will be useful at this stage to discuss how apartheid was established and consolidated, before going on to the question of contradictions within the white ruling class of South Africa.

The conflict between the European immigrant minority and the Africans in South Africa, which started over the land question and is still a major clash, has developed to a high level that is reckoned to threaten world peace. When the Europeans wrested the land from the Africans, they also automatically assumed political and economic power. As will be illustrated, to maintain this power the minority had to suppress the majority by force and denial of the basic human rights and by adopting the policy of maximum separation of the non-Europeans from the ruling Europeans. In order to implement and consolidate the policy of apartheid the National Party, after coming to power in 1948, enacted the following laws which embody some of the most important features of apartheid.

The Prohibition of Mixed Marriages Act, 1949

For a very long time in the Cape there was no law prohibiting mixed marriages. Many people in fact were proud to be of mixed race. The Dutch settler Van Meerhof was actually rewarded with a higher rank for being the first of his country-men to marry a Khoi woman. The settlers, it must be re-membered, did not initially bring women with them. The population of the Cape was (and still by and large is) a mixture of Dutch, Malay, Griqua, Coloured and African. White racial purity there was not only mythical but a ridicu-lous concept. Discrimination became more vigorous as African labour became increasingly necessary for white profit. And when cheap labour and poverty became sy-nonymous with black, then whites claimed racial purity and moreover innate supremacy. It was the Hertzog government which in 1927 enacted the Immorality Act that outlawed extra-marital relations between Europeans and Africans. The white leaders feared infiltration or erosion of their authority through mixed marriages. If mixed marriages had been allowed, the mere mixing of races at such a level would have contributed to exposing the myth of white racial superiority; the more races mix, the more they get to know and under-stand each other, and that is clearly contrary to the policy of consolidating apartheid. Then in 1949, The Prohibiton of Mixed Marriages Act prescribed criminal penalties for the Europeans and Coloureds who might choose to marry.

The Population Registration Act, 1950

Under this act every person must have an identity certificate stating whether he or she is white, native or coloured. Every-one is classified according to race. On 21st February 1950,

Dr Malan said: "a national register is the basis of the whole policy of apartheid."(15)The population of South Africa comprises the following:

	Urban(1970)	Rural(1970)	Mid-1972 estimate
Africans	4,989,371	10,068,581	16,217,000
Coloureds	1,494,490	523,963	2,144,000
Asians	535,536	81,900	668,000
Whites	3,257,805	493,523	3,960,000
			22,989,000

The Africans are the majority both in the urban and rural areas. The African population doubles every twenty years. From the 1970 census figures, 53.3 per cent of the total African population resides in the "white" cities, and from 1960 to 1970 this African population increased in the "white" cities by 1,200,000. It is logical, although contrary to the policy of racial separation, that the number of Africans in the "white" urban areas should increase since the economy is based on black labour. Indeed, following the "unrest" in the African townships, in Johannesburg particularly, in 1976, a plan was mooted by the government to give Africans the right to ownership of property within these townships.

The Group Areas Act, 1950

The purpose of the Group Areas Act, 1950 is to maintain and legalise the principle of different residential areas for the various racial groups. The idea is to restrict each racial group to particular areas. For instance, if area A is classified as "white", members of other racial groups cannot legally own property or land or reside in area A. Before the enactment of this act, there were other laws which restricted the movement of races or their ability to acquire immovable property in different parts of the country. These were laws like the

27

Natives' Land Act of 1913, the Native (Urban Areas) Act of 1923, the Native Trust and Land Act of 1936. As a result of these laws the African majority can legally and permanently reside in only 13.4 per cent of the land area — and this is put forward as a permanent solution. The land laws and the Bantu Authorities Act of 1951 form the legal basis of the Bantustan policy, to which we shall return later.

Bantu Authorities Act, 1951

The aim of the Bantu Authorities Act of 1951 was to reclassify and separate Africans into small ethnic groups and to prevent them from grouping on a national basis. Under the act Africans have tribal councils comprising a chief and advisers for administering their local affairs. Regional councils of representatives from a number of tribal councils have some powers on issues like schools, soil conservation, control of stock diseases, afforestation, hospitals, roads and other areas approved by the government. Above the regional councils are territorial councils, responsible to the Department of Native Affairs. The act gives Africans power to run their own affairs in their areas under the supervision of the white government of South Africa. It places the chiefs and headmen in an awkward situation, since they must try to retain the confidence and trust of their people and yet be responsible to the white authorities who represent white interests which are diametrically opposed to those of the black people.

The Reservation of Separate Amenities Act, 1953

Facilities for different races under this law are separate and unequal. Entrances to railway stations, post offices and other public places are segregated for the various races. Trains, buses and benches in public parks are similarly divided, many marked "For Europeans Only" or "For Non-Whites Only". Again, the Reservation of Separate Amenities Act of

1953 adds to the body of legislation keeping the contact between people of different races at its barest minimum. Behind this policy is the argument that social intercourse of two races would eventually lead to the cultural disappearance of the two races and that in such a situation sooner rather than later the minority race, which controls economic power, would lose that economic power as a racial group.

The Bantu Education Act, 1953

The Bantu Education Act of 1953 is aimed at maintaining the subordinate position of the African in South Africa, reinforcing the policy of keeping the African as tribal as possible. Thus there is great stress placed on African vernaculars as languages of instruction. The English-speaking churches believe that the Africans should be given a European type of education in order to "civilise, Christianise and westernise them", while the Afrikaners and the Dutch Reformed Churchmen consider that the kind of education Africans need is one which will preserve their "tribal identity" and prevent them from reaching an academic level where they may be in a position to challenge the white man. For Africans, practical training is favoured by the authorities, rather than academic education.

Where modern capitalists would recommend that the education of the general population be geared to the promotion of the socio-economic development plan, the National Party would argue that since the non-Europeans are the majority, such an educational policy would lead eventually to domination of the economy by the Africans and thus destroy "the white Christian civilisation — apartheid" which it is trying to build. (16) So racial segregation is rigidly enforced in the educational field and the allocation of educational resources reflects the overall policy; Punt Janson, Deputy Minister of Bantu Education, gave parliament the breakdown of allocations (per head per annum) between the racial groups in September 1974 as: (17)

Blacks:	R28.5
Coloureds:	R91.2 (primary schools), and
	R124.52 (secondary schools)
Indians:	R183.49
Whites:	R483.75

There are three African universities, while there are ten for whites: in 1974 85.5 per cent of South African university students were white, 7 per cent were black.(18)

The Native Labour (Settlement of Disputes) Act, 1953

This law develops the Industrial Conciliation Act of 1937 Africans are forbidden to form legally recognised trade unions, and there is no just machinery for settling industrial disputes. Under the act only whites are considered employees, while non-whites are servants and non-employees; strikes by blacks are therefore illegal. (Despite these prohibitions, South Africa has the second highest incidence of strikes in Africa.) The 1937 act also included the principle of job reservation.

Under the Native Labour (Settlement of Disputes) Act of 1953 regional Native Labour Committees were established, composed of Africans operating under a European chairman called the Native Labour Relations Officer. The African members of the committees and the Native Labour Relations Officer are all appointed by the Minister of Labour. The committees deal with disputes between workers and employer; if they fail to resolve a dispute, the case goes to the Central Native Labour Board, made up of Europeans only and appointed by the minister. Above this is the National Board.

The government feared that if Africans were allowed to form recognised trade unions, these unions could be used for political purposes; if they were recognised, this would be an incentive for them to grow to a point where it might be impossible to control them, and thus the "white Christian civilisation" based on the effective separation and classification of "races and tribes" could eventually collapse. The Minister of Labour, B.J. Shoeman, explained in the House of Assembly on August 4th 1953: "It is obvious that the stronger the native trade union movement should become, the more dangerous it would be to the Europeans in South Africa — we would probably be committing race suicide if we give them that incentive." (19)

The South African government is determined to withold all political rights from urban Africans, and to this end the Prime Minister, B.J. Vorster, on April 24th 1968 said: ". . . They remain there because they cannot provide employment for themselves. But the fact that you employ these people, does not place you under any obligation to grant them political rights in your Parliament. Surely the fact that you work for a man does not give you the right to run his affairs? . . . It is true that there are blacks working for us. They will continue to work for us for generations, in spite of the ideal we have to separate them completely. . . The fact of the matter is this: we need them, because they work for us, but after all, we pay them for their work. . . But the fact that they work for us can never. . . entitle them to claim political rights. Not now, nor in the future. . . under no circumstances can we grant them those political rights in our own territory, neither now nor ever."

The wage gap between African and European is widest and narrowest in the mining and manufacturing industries respectively. As the table below shows, the gap is widening, instead of narrowing:

	Ratio of White to African Wages	
	1969	1971
Mining	18.9:1	19.9:1
	1960	
Manufacturing	5.3:1	6:1

	All races	Whites (in thousands)	Africans	Coloureds/ Asians
1 Agriculture, forestry & fishing	1,980	115	1,680	185
2 Mining	676	63	606	7
3 Manufacturing & construction	1,539	336	882	321
4 Wholesale & retail trade	452	193	187	72
5 Transport & communications	279	149	110	20
6 Public authorities	649	238	336	75
7 Other services	1,465	301	990	174
Totals:	7,040	1,395	4,791	854

As has been indicated, from 1948 to 1953 the National Party government enacted enough legislation to effectively implement its apartheid policy during its first five years in office. The laws mentioned — by no means a complete list of those passed — give a picture of the nature of apartheid's legal base. All these laws emphasise racial separateness, distinctiveness and differentiation. The Afrikaner nationalists in power would like to eliminate or at least effectively control the kind of contact between Europeans and non-Europeans about which *Die Transvaler* wrote on February 27th 1957: "It is not so much the overwhelming numbers of the non-Europeans but the destruction of the feeling of difference and otherness which is the great danger for the preservation of the European and his civilisation in this multi-racial land. As long as liberalistic bishops and canons, professors, students and politicians can freely attend church and hold meetings and socials together, apartheid will be infriged to its marrow."

Bantustans

The policy of apartheid divides Africans into Bantustans on the basis of tribe against their will and unites all white people as a dominant European bloc under the leadership of the Afrikaners through the National Party. According to the Bantu Homelands Citizenship Act of 1970, all Africans, whether they live in the Bantu Homelands or not, belong to their designated homelands. Africans are supposed to be temporary sojourners in the urban areas and other parts of the country outside the reserves or the Bantu Homelands, which cover an area of 13.4 per cent of South Africa, as opposed to the remainder of the country which is reserved for whites by law. The table on page shows that Bantustans are made up of scattered pieces of land. These Bantu Homelands or reserves or Bantustans are ten in number, to be consolidated into 24 areas. Only Basotho Qwaqua and South Ndebele are single entities; the other eight are each composed of several unconnected fragments. The Bantustans are not economically viable and are too small and poor to contain all the people who are designated their citizens. They are conceived as subsidiary units of white South Africa.

There is widespread African opposition to the Bantustan policy in South Africa. The arguments against them, as expressed by the South African Student Organisation (SASO) in 1972, are these:(21)

"1. That these are institutions of oppression designed to cheat people into believing that they have communicating links with Pretoria;
2. that whites have no right to balkanise the country and allocate any percentage of it to blacks;
3. that artificial division of blacks into ethnic groups is aimed at the fragmentation of the struggle by the blacks towards emancipation;
4. that participation in Bantustan politics is merely aimed at cheating the outside world into believing that there is

"Homeland"	Ethnic Group	Territory (in hectares)	Number of	Population of the Bantustan, 1970 (in thousands)	Population of the ethnic group 1970 (in thousands)	Per cent of population in Bantustan
Transkei	Xhosa	3,672,212	2	1,651	3,930	55.0
Ciskei	Xhosa	918,547	17 (to be consolidated into 4)	510		
Kwazulu	Zulu	3,144,421	48 (reduction to 10 planned)	2,057	4,026	51.1
Lebowa	North Sotho (or Sepedi)	2,214,086	15 (to be consolidated into 6)	899	1,604	56.0
Venda	Venda	604,355	3 (to be consolidated into 2)	239	358	66.8
Gazan Kulu	Shangaan (or Tsonga)	667,292	5 (to be consolidated into 3)	234	737	31.8
Bophuthat-swana	Tswana	3,754,018	19 (to be consolidated into 6)	600	1,719	34.9
Basotho-qwaqwa	South Sotho (or Seshoeshoe)	45,742	1	24	1,452	1.7
Swazi	Swazi	211,807	2	82	499	16.4

Note: By 1965 it was also intended to establish a "homeland" for Ndebele (not included in the table).
Source: H.E. Mr. Edwin Ogebe Ogbu (Nigeria), Chairman, United Nations Unit on Apartheid, New York, 1975.

validity in the multi-national policy of the white nationalists;

5. that the whole philosophy of separate development is a 'solution mooted by the same people who have created the problem.' "

The following quotations further illuminate the true intentions behind the apartheid scheme:

1. "The Bantu Homelands . . . will be areas which to a large extent . . . are dependent on basic incomes earned (in) the adjoining white territory. In that case the whole of the threat to the white areas falls away." (Dr Hendrik Verwoerd, House of Assembly, June 29, 1959).
2. "I have confidence in the mass of our Bantu, with the exception of a small group of agitators . . . We are trying to establish well-disposed little black neighbouring states . . ." (Dr Hendrik Verwoerd, 1962).
3. "The Bantustans are a chain of labour reservoirs where people are held in a state of compulsory unemployment until the white economy wants them." (*Rand Daily Mail*, August 18, 1973).
4. "Under the Bantu authorities . . . you will be able to lead the people in a true sense. You will be able to tell them, not to ask them, what to do. This is an important point." (Secretary for Native Affairs, 1963).
5. "At least half of South Africa's black population can never be accommodated in the Homelands. The year 2020 would therefore see 30 million Africans living, without political rights, in 'white South Africa'." (Professor David Kriek, University of South Africa, 8 April 1976).
6. "Black work seekers will increase by 220,000 a year in 1977-1980. Just over half, 114,200, will be in the Homelands. During the last three years, job opportunities for Homelands blacks rose by only about 65,000 a year, and of those nearly 37,000 were *outside the Homelands* in the 'border industries' (owned by whites, designed to employ

Homeland blacks). If this rate of job creation continues only 65% of Homelands work-seekers will get jobs in or near their 'homes'. Since South Africa is suffering a recession the rate of job creation is expected to go down." (*Report on Bantustan Economies* by the South African Bureau for Economic Research (Benbo), June 1976).

7. "The Council of Ministers in the Organization of African Unity meeting in its ninth extraordinary session, in Dar-es-Salaam from 7 to 10 April 1975 . . . decided to reiterate its condemnation and rejection of any Bantustan policy and practice and call on all United Nations Member-States to desist from establishing any contacts with the Homeland 'leaders' . . . . " (UN Notes and Documents, No. 19/75).

Professor Julian R. Friedman has given a useful summary of the functions that apartheid performs:[22]

"(a) to sustain among Europeans a personal and communal sense of superiority;
 (b) to stereotype and denigrate the capabilities of Africans, Coloureds, and Asians;
 (c) to protect status and jobs for Europeans on the basis of colour regardless of integrity and ability;
 (d) to sharpen stratification of the society to the degree that a caste system can be maintained;
 (e) to retard life-chances and restrict opportunities for the advancement of Africans, Coloureds and Asians;
 (f) to deny the validity of the principle of equality in relations among people."

Apartheid is maintained by the following measures:[22]

"(a) destroying the will among Africans, Coloureds and Asians as well as the European opposition to resist the imposition of apartheid;
 (b) immobilising Africans, Coloureds, and Asians as far as political activities are concerned;

(c) destroying independent leadership among Africans, Coloureds, and Asians;
(d) curtailing circulation of ideas and information of a political nature;
(e) isolating Africans from external support, as well as cross-community assistance;
(f) unifying the European communities against the common enemy, under white Nationalist leadership;
(g) magnifying European 'authority' and engendering the confidence of the whites in the regime;
(h) countering 'liberalistic' tendencies."

Although the non-white people are the major victims of the policy of apartheid, in practice, certain basic liberties of the Europeans have perforce been progressively curtailed in order to maintain apartheid through the following restrictions on: (22)

"(a) freedom to choose an area of residence;
(b) freedom not to be classified and identified by 'race' ;
(c) freedom to marry a person of one's own choice;
(d) freedom to engage in personal and private conduct as a consenting adult;
(e) freedom to engage in business or practice professions in areas of one's choice;
(f) freedom to assemble or even visit with friends and other persons;
(g) freedom to select candidates for the Parliament and other legislative bodies;
(h) freedom to travel throughout South Africa;
(i) freedom to enjoy a speedy trial upon detention;
(j) freedom to enjoy a privacy of one's home without invasion by the police;
(k) freedom of speech on public policy;
(l) freedom to travel abroad;

(m) freedom to contribute to charities of one's choice and assist the needy;
(n) freedom to read publications;
(o) freedom to attend churches of one's preference;
(p) freedom to bargain collectively on the labour market;
(q) freedom to assign employees to jobs and tasks;
(r) freedom to house employees on one's own property;
(s) freedom to negotiate the sale or purchase of real property; and
(t) freedom to select students for schools and universities."

Having given the broad historical context, we return to examine in more detail the contradictions within the white ruling class. The table on page 35 shows how the white electorate of South Africa has voted since 1948, and indicates the conflicts other than the Afrikaner-English dichotomy that exist among the whites. These tendencies are reflected in the mass media of the country, as will be shown later.

Within the Afrikaner community, apart from the National Party there is also the more extreme Hersigte Nationale Party (HNP). The HNP was formed by a group of Afrikaners under the leadership of Dr Albert Hertzog in 1969 as a result of the power struggle within the National Party. It is a conflict between the verligtes, the more "enlightened" and liberal, and the verkramptes, ultra-bigoted Afrikaners who reject all forms of change in South Africa. These are the two centres of power within the National Party and the Afrikaner community. Most of the verkramptes, in the interests of Afrikaner unity, remain in the National Party, -instead of defecting to the HNP. The policies of the Vorster government vacilitate between the verligtes and the verkramptes — a technique which has helped to keep the HNP at bay. The verligtes press for a more outward-looking foreign policy, ie friendly relations with African states as a way of preventing those states from supporting African liberation movements; they accommodate pro-apartheid non-Afrikaner whites in order to strengthen white power in South Africa; and they approve of giving more rights to the Africans in the urban areas. All these attitudes are bitterly opposed by the verkramptes, who believe that liberalism and flexibility are a great threat to the survival of Afrikaner power in South Africa.

The conflict and confusion in the Afrikaner camp surfaced more openly as a result of the 1976 struggles in Soweto and other African and Coloured areas in South Africa. Afrikaner intellectuals and newspapers are the leading exponents of the ideas of the verligtes. Some, like Professor Dreyer Kruger of Rhodes University (23) have gone as far as to point out — as Professor Kruger did in an address to the Afrikaans Society in September 1976 — that the Afrikaner is betraying himself by not caring for the welfare of black people, that Afrikaner power is doomed, and so much the better too. He commented that Afrikaans culture had become intertwined with continued political dominance and that inevitably the Afrikaner would lose. The *Sunday Times* of South Africa devoted a page to printing Professor Kruger's speech.

Professor Tjaart van der Walt, Chairman of the influential Afrikaans Calvinistiese Beweging (Calvinistic Movement) urged the government to make fundamental changes in the country's political, economic and social system.(23) A Professor of Philosophical Jurisprudence, J. van der Vyver, has also argued that the Afrikaner must permit all the other national groups in South Africa equal rights and privileges, or else he will destroy his own freedom.(23) The pro-government *Die Vaderland*(23) appealed to the Afrikaners not to return to the "laager" (the defence encampments of early Boer settlers) and to understand that many aspects of apartheid were impossible to implement, and that the blacks would continue to resist. The Johannesburg *Transvaaler,* another pro-government newspaper(23), warned that the time for window-dressing and evolutionary development had run out. *Die Bleed.* also pro-government, declared that without an appreciable increase in the pace of change the future

39

looks desolate for the ruling party and the country as a whole.(23)

In November 1976 Mr Piet Cillie, Editor of Cape Town's pro-government *Die Burger,* commenting on the African struggles in Soweto and other parts of the country, suggested in his weekly column that Africans in the urban areas of South Africa who did not belong to any Bantustan should be given full rights in a common constitutional structure with whites. Mr Cillie's appeal for equal rights goes quite contrary to official government policy.(24)

All these instances represent the escalation of the conflict and confusion in the Afrikaner ruling elite, which, as will be shown later, reflects the growing power and the new level of strength of the liberation struggle in South Africa within an international situation which is unfavourable to the continuation of racist oppression in the country. It is a crisis which can only end with the complete liberation and social transformation of the socio-economic system in SouthAfrica.

The United Party,* representing the interests of the English and of other moderate elements in the white community, has been the main opposition part ? in South Africa since 1948. It enjoys the support of richer people in the white community than the National Party. Thus Verwoerd in 1951 when he was prime minister declared that "with the help of the big capitalists, the United Party is trying to crush nationalism in South Africa with gold."(25)

The policy of the National Party is similar to that of the United Party on English-Afrikaner relations and on white-black relations. On English-Afrikaner relations each party policy stresses ". . .equality of the Afrikaans-speaking and the English-speaking sections of the community, coupled with the recognition and appreciation by either section of the distinctive cultural heritage of the other."(26) This has not eliminated competition between the two groups, since each wishes to see itself in the ascendancy.

On white-black relations, the policy of the two parties is

*As the book was going to press the United Party merged with the Democratic Party under the name "New Republic Party" and the Progressive Reform Party was joined by 5 MPs from the United Party and changed its name to "Progressive Federal Party" in September, 1977. Further re-alignment of forces seemed inevitable.

that blacks should live under the "Christian trusteeship of the European races" and both parties would want to "cultivate a spirit of goodwill and mutual trust between Europeans and non-Europeans"(26) based on a permanent senior-junior relationship. While the National Party believes in enforcing direct and outright discrimination against the non-white population, the United Party advocates milder forms of segregation. Following criticism that the United Party's programme was similar to that of the National Party on the non-European question, the United Party Congress of November 1954 redefined party policy as: "sincere willingness and desire to share Western civilisation in practice with all non-whites who have developed the capacity for taking joint responsibility for our future well-being in this sub-continent . . . the Native should gradually be given a more definite and secure place within the orbit of our Western way of life."(27) This, as the United Party sees it, is the only guarantee for maintaining white leadership in South Africa.

Within the English-speaking community there is also the more liberal Progressive Reform Party which broke away from the United Party in 1959 (under the name Progressive Party). It took its present name in 1975 when it merged with another dissident group of United Party members. It enjoys the sympathy of most of the English-language press. In the 1961 election the English-language press supported the United Party against the National Party merely because the Progressive Reform Party did not have sufficient support to be a serious challenge to the National Party. The bulk of the English press, however, hoped that a time would come when the politics of the Progressive Reform Party would be acceptable to the white electorate. The Progressive Reform Party is backed by big business, including the influential Mr Harry Oppenheimer, chairman of the mighty Anglo-American Corporation. In 1976 the party had twelve members in the South African parliament. A re-alignment of anti-apartheid white politicians aimed at strengthening the opposition to the National Party is foreseen as a logical development.

The Progressive Reform Party advocates multi-racialism; a qualitative franchise; one parliament for all races; and the spread and maintenance of white civilisation. Its position is too radical for most whites and too liberal for the black majority. But it remains a powerful factor in a pre-liberated South Africa. The differences between the National Party, the United Party, the Hersigte National Party and the Progressive Reform Party are not on fundamental issues like white supremacy, but rather on the methods of consolidating the system. The main conflict therefore is between the deprived voiceless black majority and the white minority who control parliament and the economy of the country. The conflict between the Afrikaners and the English-speaking people of South Africa is a minor but important one. The Afrikaner-English dimension, or the conservative versus the liberal issue, represents a contradiction in the white camp which can be important during the collapse of minority rule. In a struggle between A and B, contradictions within B's camp can be of great service to A and vice versa. The more the white minority as a ruling power is divided, the more the victory of the revolutionary forces is hastened. The more the revolutionary forces intensify the struggle, the weaker and more divided the ruling power becomes. The adage "united we stand, divided we fall" is relevant here: the further the conflict between the Afrikaners and the English (or between the conservative and the liberal) escalates, the more useful that conflict can be to those who seek radical political change in South Africa. By being owned or representing various white factions, the media are a mirror through which contradictions are revealed and the liberationists are able to keep abreast of the development of those contradictions in the system they seek to change.

HOW THE WHITE ELECTORATE OF SOUTH AFRICA HAS VOTED SINCE 1948*

	1948	1953	1958	1961	1966	1970	1974
Total number of seats	153	159	163	156	170	166	169
National Party							
Votes polled	401,834	598,718	642,069	370,431	776,766	820,968	636,585
Number and % of seats won	79(52%)	94(59%)	103(63%)	105(67%)	126(76%)	117(70%)	112(72%)
United Party							
Votes polled	524,230	576,474	503,639	302,875	490,971	561,647	363,459
Number and % of seats won	65(42%)	57(36%)	53(33%)	45(29%)	39(23%)	47(28%)	41(24%)
Progressive Party (formed 1959)							
Votes polled				69,042	41,065	51,760	58,768
Number and % of seats won				1(1%)	1(1%)	1(1%)	6(4%)
National Union							
Votes polled				35,903			
Number and % of seats won				1(1%)			
Herstigte Nasionale Party							
Votes polled						53,763	39,568
Number and % of seats won						0	0
Democratic Party (formed 1973)							
Votes polled							10,449
Number and % of seats won							0
Afrikaner Party							
Votes polled	41,885						
Number and % of seats won	9(6%)						
Native representatives	3	3	3	abolished			
Coloured representatives		4	4	4	4	abolished	

*These statistics are taken from Julian Friedman's *Basic Facts on the Republic of South Africa and the Policy of Apartheid*, UN Unit on Apartheid, Department of Political and Security Council Affairs, New York, August 1974, page 21.

The Media

Radio

By controlling parliament the Nationalist Party controls the South African Broadcasting Corporation (SABC) which is a statutory body established under the Broadcasting Act of 1936.(28) SABC operates under a government-appointed board of governors. Parity between English and Afrikaans language programme running-time was its priority. During the Second World War, however, many SABC employees volunteered to join the army and were replaced by Afrikaners, who regarded the war as an English concern and were reluctant to become involved. When the Nationalist Party won the elections in 1948, it was evident that the Afrikaners would dominate both the board of governors and the staff of the SABC, and in 1950 the company stopped relaying BBC news broadcasts. The SABC consistently attacks the English-language press and, contrary to its original charter, does not seek to be impartial. It openly propagates the policies of the Nationalist Party government.

In May 1950 Springbok Radio was established under the auspices of the SABC as a commercial channel based in Johannesburg. Springbok Radio managed to get most of its advertising from the businesses controlled by English-speaking people. This meant that it displayed a greater British economic influence, which many Afrikaners resented. As a result, the Afrikaans daily newspaper, *Die Transvaler*, stated that the "service was exposing Afrikaner homes to a blast of foreign influence."(29)

There is also Radio Bantu, set up for Africans in 1952 under the auspices of the SABC, when the government felt the need to popularise the policy of apartheid. In 1964 there were seven separate services under Radio Bantu broadcasting in the Xhosa language in Cape Province; South Sotho in the Orange Free State; Tswana in Northern Cape and Western

Transvaal; North Sotho in Central Transvaal; Zulu in Natal and south-eastern Transvaal; and in the north-eastern Transvaal the Tsonga and Venda services. The programmes are transmitted via low transistorised FM portables. At the outset, Radio Bantu was limited to 30 minutes once a week, until in the 60s the regime felt the need for highpowered propaganda to be spread among the Africans. This was the result of the Sharpeville upheaval of 1960 which culminated in the shooting of more than 83 Africans and a general intensifying of the struggle against racist exploitation.

For Soweto Msakazo radio station has existed since the mid-50s. The Pan Africanist Congress of Azania (PAC) infiltrated the station and broadcast an appeal for support for the demonstrations of March 21, 1960. This led to very close official surveillance, after sackings of all but one member of the black staff. One announcer, Stanley Mokoena, was gaoled on Robben Island from 1963 to 1974.

White regional FM commercial services also exist: Radio Highveld, Radio Good Hope and Radio Port Natal. In 1972 medium or short wave services were available to the whole of South Africa and 97.5 per cent of the country could receive the FM services. In 1971 there were 1,856,119 licence holders in South Africa and more than 40,000 in South West Africa.

Radio RSA, the Voice of South Africa, which started broadcasting in the 1960s, has world-wide external services today. It gives priority to news and stories unfavourable to progressive African states, socialist countries and the liberation struggle internationally. Racial incidents which might show that there is racial prejudice or ethnic discrimination in these countries is given prominent coverage.

Television
South Africa introduced television broadcasting in 1976 on a non-commercial basis. It was planned to have different channels in line with apartheid policy, with Africans not being permitted to tune in to white channels. Licences to

manufacture television sets were to be restricted to five companies. One of these companies is partly owned by Perskor, on whose board six cabinet members sit.

South Africa has lagged far behind other industrially developed countries in embracing television broadcasting. Although closed-circuit systems were in use as early as 1936, no broadcast television was allowed. By June 1971 closed-circuit television had been permitted by the Postmaster General for medical, educational and industrial applications. During the early years of the National Party, the South African government categorically stated that broadcast television would not be introduced.(30) The government feared the possible effects of television on the population: since most programmes would be British or American, television would enhance the influence of the English-speaking community of South Africa, which comprises about 40 per cent of the total white population. Foreign films and programmes would undermine the government's efforts to prevent liberal, permissive or progressive ideas from influencing the population.

Ivor Benson in a chapter on "Rhodesia's TV Lesson for South Africa"(33) echoed the views of the South African government when he stated that if broadcast television were to be introduced in South Africa, then it should be strictly state-controlled and should not be allowed to show films with multi-racial casts of actors which undermine the ideas and standards that have shaped the South African way of life.

In October 1971 the government, surprisingly, declared that South Africa would establish a national television system in 1976, that the German telefunken PAL system would be adopted and that it would be strictly controlled by the Ministry of Posts and Telegraphs.(30) It was estimated that television would be brought to 75 per cent of the white community, 60 per cent of the Coloureds and 84 per cent of the Asians. After these percentages were achieved, the Bantu TV for Africans would be introduced.

The Printed Media

As has already been indicated, the South African press reflects the Afrikaner/English politics of the country. The English-language press, supporting the ideas of the United Party and the Progressive Reform Party, is owned by big business interests. The Afrikaans press, supporting the ruling National Party and in the main upholding the apartheid policy, was established later than its English-language counterparts. As Francis Williams has observed, the South African English papers did not "establish themselves as independent forces, sympathetic to, but not controlled by the expanding commercial interests in their society . . . They were the direct instruments of financial and commercial power springing fully armed into the arena: the ancillaries of commerce, not its mentors."(32)

Today there are four main newspaper groups in South Africa: the Argus group (the biggest), the South African Associatied Newspapers (SAAN), the Nasionale Pers, and the Afrikaanse Pers. The Argus Group by 1974 owned seven dailies, and four weeklies. It had a 31 per cent controlling interest in SAAN, which owns four dailies and two weeklies. Seven of the eleven dailies have special weekend editions. The Argus group has interests throughout Southern Africa; the Anglo-American Corporation, Rand Mines Group and the Johannesburg Consolidated Investment Company are the mining finance houses which control the Argus Printing and Publishing Company; four of the eight directors of the Argus company are nominees of the mining companies.(33) The Argus group also sponsors newspapers for the non-whites: the *Cape Herald* is published for the Coloureds in the Cape, the *Post* for the Indians in Natal, and the *World* for the Africans throughout the republic. These are produced in English, the only paper published for Africans in an African language being *Ilanga Lase Natal* in Zulu. The non-white press concentrates on sport, crime, sex, and cannot be the political mouthpiece of the African population without getting into trouble with the authorities. The non-white press was not created for that purpose either.

The Afrikaans-language press is owned mainly by the Dagbreek Trust and Nasionale Pers, both of which are loyal supporters of the National Party. Both have cabinet ministers on their boards of directors. In 1973 the Dagbreek Trust had the following gracing its board: B.J. Shoeman, Minister of Transport (chairman); M.C. Botha, Minister of Bantu Administration and Development (vice-chairman); N.J. Diederichs, Minister of Finance (later State President); Dr H. Muller, Minister of Foreign Affairs; M. Viljoen, Minister of Labour, Posts and Telegraphs; C.P. Mulder, Minister of Information, Social Welfare and Immigration; J. de Klerk, President of the Senate. The Nasionale Pers has, among its directors, P.W. Botha, Minister of Defence, and P.C. Pelsner, Minister of Justice and Pensions.

In September 1976 a new morning English-language newspaper, *The Citizen*, was launched by Mr Louis Luyt, a multi-millionaire, who put £8 million into the venture. The aim of the paper is to support apartheid and challenge the other English-language papers, especially the *Rand Daily Mail,* which has a black readership estimated at 30,000. *The Citizen* started with one black reporter, whereas the *Rand Daily Mail* has 11. Mr Louis Luyt is motivated by white nationalist patriotism rather than profit. Production costs are rising, while the downturn in the economy and the advent of television are adversely affecting newspaper revenues from advertising and cutting circulation.

Ownership and Content
None of the media can publish or broadcast material undermining the fundamental principles of their owners or the elements upon which they depend financially without precipitating a crisis in their relationship. The South African mass media have vested interests in maintaining the status quo as "responsible" white media. To survive profitably they need economic stability within the socio-economic system of

which they are an integral part. For instance, the English-language press cannot readily initiate a vigorous campaign in support of higher wages for the African labour force, nor can they advocate peaceful African strikes and other forms of action considered by government and the industrialists to be economic sabotage.(34)

However, the situation allows the media enough freedom to criticise directly or indirectly certain features of the system which are not fundamental to it. The media have recommended some social reforms and exposed certain facts, sometimes to the annoyance or embarrassment of the government. An examination of the cases brought against journalists in South Africa and the grounds on which they are arrested and convicted shows that any criticism of the system must be mild and not a direct assault upon the principle of white supremacy(35). But even criticisms of the excesses of a system can be healthy for it. They can have the effect of improving, and thereby consolidating, that system which in fact should be changed rather than consolidated. Criticisms aimed at making a society function more smoothly (ie aimed at minimising conflict between rich and poor, between master and servant, between black and white — without attacking the basis of the conflict or relationship or without advocating complete change) show the mass media performing a functional role.(36) Instead of attacking the nature and purpose of the law itself, the tendency is to attack the crude way in which the law is implemented.

Contrary to the thesis advanced by Elaine Potter(37) that "between 1948 and 1958 the English language press became an 'external' opposition whilst the Afrikaans language press, as an institution within the ranks of Government, constituted an internal opposition", the press in South Africa as a social institution is an expression of a system of domination and an instrument for reinforcing it.(38) The mass media represent the hopes and aspirations of the people who own, advertise in and publish them. They represent the forces of status quo, ie the continuation of white supremacy. As we have seen, the English-language press for many years encouraged people to vote for the United Party whose programme does not include the extension of political rights to all the inhabitants of South Africa. The press's role as an opposition is indirect and minimal under the circumstances.

The Afrikaans-language press, the South African Broadcasting Corporation and the television service advocate the policies of the ruling National Party. Differences of opinion exist on how best to maintain white dominance, rather than on how to eradicate the system itself. The main differences between the two groups may be seen under the two slogans: "integration" under white leadership and civilisation or "complete separation" under white leadership.

While the press performs its function as an instrument of oppression and reinforcing that system, it nevertheless has to inform the white ruling class about all the developments and views of people internally and externally which affect the wellbeing of the socio-economic system in South Africa. But the mass media by their very nature are public, so the whole nation is informed — including the black majority and others who support liberation. Even if the press may be openly biased in favour of the status quo, the white minority will still need to know exactly what is happening so that it can plan its strategy accordingly. What it needs to know is the work and views of the liberationists, their allies and sympathisers inside the country and outside. It also needs to be appraised of the effects of the activities of the whole opposition movement on the system. The press is obliged to inform the white* community. The press becomes an extremely sensitive area in politics. When the oppressed and their supporters get the news, they read between the lines; they learn to know the weaknesses of the system; who its enemies are, how desperate it may be; and they form a clear picture of the mind of the ruling class. So, in the process of informing the white community and its government, the press informs the black community too. Anything that disheartens the racist system gives encouragement to the oppressed. The press, because of its mass character, cannot be hidden from the oppressed and therefore unintentionally and indirectly contributes to the process of liberation. By being unsubtly and publicly hostile to the ideas and movement of liberation, the press and the state's propaganda machine contribute to the raising of consciousness among the oppressed majority. It makes them more bitter and determined. The oppressed also listen to foreign radio broadcasts and read literature smuggled into South Africa, the content of which may be hostile to oppression and supporting liberation. The people compare the views and slanted reports against their liberation with the information they receive in favour of their emancipation. They find that they have sufficient information to lead them to more revolutionary conclusions. They find that their struggle is never a hopeless cause. There is always something to boost their morale.

As the circulation figures on the table on pages 44 and 45 show, the English-language press has the highest circulation. Those papers also have considerable black readerships. Since they form about 80 per cent of the total population, the number of black readers is bound to increase. The English press, being dependent on advertising and circulation, finds that black readers are important for their survival. As an indication of their economic importance: it was reported in 1976 that black people buy 91% of bicycles in South Africa; 84% of the gin sold; 73% of the instant coffee; and 64% of the chocolates on the market.(39)

Largely because of these statistics the Afrikaans press, especially *Rapport* and *Die Burger*, has become increasingly interested in black circulation. In fact, the English press, particularly the *Rand Daily Mail*, has often been accused of being strongly anti-apartheid in order to attract black readers. But then, as has been illustrated earlier, the Afrikaans papers themselves which started as mere party organs have begun to be vigorous in criticising the excesses of apartheid. Coverage of views and activities of opposition whites and of developments within the black community has become broader than before.

1976 CIRCULATION FIGURES OF
SOUTH AFRICAN NEWSPAPERS (40)

ARGUS GROUP

	Daily	Weekend	Weekly
The Star	184,110	115,245	
Cape Argus	108,826	138,671	
World	131,190	187,643	
Daily News	95,888	38,373	
Friend	7,744		
Diamond Fields Advertiser	7,559		
Pretoria News	27,052	12,584	
Sunday Tribune			149,862
Cape Herald			82,830
Ilanga Lasenatal			77,595
Post			42,517

SOUTH AFRICAN ASSOCIATED NEWSPAPERS
(in which the Argus Group has a 31.25% interest)

	Daily	Weekend	Weekly
Rand Daily Mail	137,363		
Eastern Province Herald	28,200		
Evening Post	24,634	46,654	
Sunday Times			487,292
Sunday Express			134,840
Financial Mail			21,000
Cape Times	68,531	88,234	

NATIONALE PERS GROUP

	Daily	Weekend	Weekly
Die Burger	68,325	80,225	
Oosterlig	11,610		
Die Volksblad	29,211	23,615	
Die Beeld	47,619		

DAGBREEK TRUST GROUP
(Afrikaanse Perse)

	Daily	Weekend	Weekly
Die Vaderland	61,000	23,900	
Hoofstad	24,000		
Financial Gazette			11,000
(Voostrekker Pers)			
Die Transvaler	63,747	48,046	
(Hoofstadpers)			
Hoofstad	24,000		
(Perskorporasie van Suid Afrika)			
Rapport			458,490
(owned equally with Nasionale Pers)			

INDEPENDENTS

Natal Mercury	67,624
Natal Witness	17,318
Daily Despatch	26,418

RHODESIAN NEWSPAPERS

	Daily	Weekend
Bulawayo Chronicle	32,615	
Sunday News		27,382
Sunday Mail		89,421
Rhodesia Herald	77,429	
Umtali Post (three times a week)	2,989	

NOTES AND REFERENCES

1. Hepple, Alex: *South Africa, a Political and Economic History*, Pall Mall Press, London, 1966, page 44.
2. Walker, Eric A.: *A History of Southern Africa*, Longmans Green, London, 1965, pages 33, 99 and 115.
3. De Kiewiet, C.W.: *A History of South Africa, Social and Economic*, Oxford University Press, London, 1966, pages 38 and 39.
4. Quoted in Lenin, V.I.: *Imperialism, the Highest Stage of Capitalism*, Foreign Languages Press, Peking, 1970, pages 93-4.
5. Walker, Eric A.: *The Great Trek*, Adam and Charles Black, London, 1965, page 16.
6. Hepple, Alex: *South Africa, a Political and Economic History*, op.cit, page 59.
7. Walker, Eric A.: *A History of Southern Africa*, op.cit, page 299.
8. Smuts, J.: "Afrikaans — Its Origin and Development", in *Encyclopaedia of Southern Africa*, Warne, London, 1965, pages 5-7.
9. Thompson, L.M.: *The Unification of South Africa*, 1902-1910, Oxford University Press, London, 1960, page 5.
10. Thompson, L.M.: ibid, page 11.
11. Wilson and Thompson: *Oxford History of South Africa*, vol 11, Oxford University Press, London, 1971, pages 325-333. Also see Hepple, Alex, *South Africa*, op.cit, pages 85-92.
12. Carter, Gwendolen M.: *The Politics of Inequality, South Africa Since 1948*, Thames and Hudson, London, 1958, page 240.
13. Quoted from *Rand Daily Mail*, June 25th 1971, in Gwendolen M. Carter, ibid, page 248.
14. Phillips, Norman: *The Tragedy of Apartheid*, Allen and Unwin, London, 1961, page 124.
15. Quoted from *Die Burger* in Gwendolen M. Carter, op cit, page 81.
16. See Houghton, Herbert F.: *The South African Economy*, Oxford University Press, London, 1964, especially from page 18 to page 24.
17. *The Star*, Johannesburg, 28th September 1974.
18. See 'Bantustan Education', an article in *Africa* magazine, London, no.48, August 1975, pages 31-33.
19. Quoted in Alex Hepple, *South Africa, a Political and Economic History*, op.cit, page 233.
20. Friedman, Julian: op.cit, page 16.
21. See *Black Review 1972*, Black Community Programmes, Durban, page 77.
22. See Friedman, Julian: op.cit, pages 25, 29, and 33.
23. See the article 'Afrikaners Sharply Divided on Political Cultural Future', by Robin Write, *International Herald Tribune*, Paris, August 5, 1976.
Also 'Afrikanerdom Adrift in a Sea of Change', by Geoffrey Taylor, *The Guardian*, London, November 15, 1976.
24. See the article: 'White Editor Urges Freedom for Blacks' by Bruce Loudon, *Daily Telegraph*, London, November 8, 1976.
25. The Johannesburg *Star*, June 1st, 1951.
26. See 'Programmes, Principles and Objectives of South African Political Parties and Groups', in Gwendolen M. Carter, op.cit, especially pages 467, 469, 472.
27. Quoted in Gwendolen Carter: op.cit, page 284.

28. Orlik, Peter B.: 'Radio in the Republic of South Africa', in *Broadcasting in Africa*, ed. Sydney W. Head, Temple University Press, Philadelphia, 1974, page 140.

29. Orlik, Peter B.: ibid, page 143, quoted from Sheila Patterson, *The Last Trek*, Routledge and Kegan Paul, London, 1957, page 156.

30. See Orlik, Peter B.: ibid, page 148.

31. See Benson, Ivor: *The Opinion Makers*, Dolphin Press, Pretoria, 1967, pages 135-141.

32. Williams, Frances: *The Right to Know: the Rise of the World Press*, Longman, London, 1969, page 48.

33. Hepple, Alex: *Press Under Apartheid*, International Defence and Aid Fund, London, 1974, page 58.

34. See Ainslie, Rosalynde, *The Press in Africa*, Gollancz, London, 1966, chapter 5 on 'Post War Southern Africa'.

35. Cases of a number of journalists detained or convicted in South Africa are analysed in the booklet *South Africa, Apartheid, Mass Media*, International Organization of Journalists, Prague, 1973;
   Also see *Apartheid: Its Effects on Education, Science, Culture and Information*, Unesco, Paris, 1967, pages 191-2.

36. See Miliband, Ralph: *The State in Capitalist Society*, Quartet Books, London, 1973, chapter 8 on the 'Process of Legitimation'.

37. Potter, Elaine: *The Press as Opposition, the Political Role of South African Newspapers*, Chatto and Windus, London, 1975, page 7.

38. Miliband, Ralph: op.cit, page 198.

39. See the article: 'The South African Press', *Index on Censorship*, Autumn 1976, London, Vol.5/Number 3, page 11.

40. See *Audit Bureau of Circulations of South Africa Ltd* figures, Johannesburg, Jan/June 1976.

Chapter 2:
Legislative and Other Restrictions on the Press

Politics is about power. In order to exercise state power it is essential first to control the state machinery. Since law is an agency of control, a system of preventing enemies and other elements in society from exercising other types of power, and emanates from the state and its machinery, it follows that the interests which control the state also control the legal system. Law is used as an instrument of policy. Its purpose is to protect the state apparatus and the power of the ruling class. When the authorities talk about law, order and peace, they mean under them and the present social, political and economic system.

In South Africa the white minority has power. It controls the state machinery and intends to keep it by force and persuasion, for ever if possible. The legal system, controlled by the ruling minority, is there to ensure — as far as it can — that no other forms of power opposed to the present set-up are exercised freely. The legal system and other state pressures are geared to making the utmost endeavour to see that individuals and institutions facilitate the smooth functioning of the social, political and economic system. They are not to be given sufficient freedom to cause difficulties to or destroy the system.

South Africa is virtually in a perpetual state of war because of the degree of polarisation between the blacks and the whites and the general insecurity of the system. It is a capitalist state based on a rigid and militant form of racialism, and the law unmistakeably reflects that state of affairs.

Ivor Benson, echoing the views of the South African government, wrote, in his book, *The Opinion Makers:*(1) "The freedom that is at stake is not that of the newspapers to supply or withold information as they think fit or to persuade as they think fit — it is the nation's freedom of access to the information it needs in order to be able to protect and promote its own vital interests. The press must be free — no one denies that — but it must be Our Press, promoting Our values and Our interests. Only such a press has any claim to the freedom to govern itself in our society." Benson does not explain what are "our values and interests". He obviously does not include in them the values and interests of the non-white majority in South Africa, nor does he include the values and interests of the people of all races who are opposed to white supremacy. In other words, "our interests" or the "public interest" means the interests of the white community, which are for the maintenance of the status quo.

It could be argued that if the South African mass media were not on the side of the forces and movements of political change, why would the government enact so many laws to control what the media may disseminate? The legislation which affects the mass media, however, itself shows that it was not enacted primarily to deal with the mass media. It is meant to protect and consolidate the system of apartheid and white rule as a whole.

South Africa's experience also proves that there is almost no limit to the number of laws a state can manufacture to protect itself from opponents who might want drastic social, political and economic changes and who might have the will and the capability to effect them. Laws to deal with the same problem can be continuously enacted and given certain conditions, factors and time-span, the system could collapse despite the immense number of laws it has bolstered itself with.

There are more than 75 laws and provincial ordinances which directly or indirectly affect the freedom of journalists, writers and other communicators to collect and disseminate information as they see fit. The laws are so rigidly defined and complex that even media people who support white supremacy find themselves constantly violating the legislation – albeit unintentionally. The nature of the laws and the way they are implemented make a mockery of the much publicised notion that there is freedom of the press in South Africa. As Richard A. Falk, Professor of International Law at Princeton university (USA) stated, after acting as an official observer for the International Commission of Jurists at a "terrorism" trial in Pretoria in 1968 :(2) "I did not appreciate beforehand that these Bantu Laws (the pass laws, the trespass laws and other regulations applied only to the African Community) are of such a character that only a relatively small percentage of the African population is in a position to comply with them at any particular time. These laws are of such complexity that someone with legal training could not easily understand the requirements of compliance."

The laws are couched in such a vague and tortuous language that the authorities can use them to arrest practically anyone at any time for anything. The system has also moved further to a point where mass arrests can be made without any explanation being offered or legal charges being brought.

Below are described only some of the most important laws affecting the press directly, as an illustration of what the situation is like: (3)

1 Bantu Administration Act (no 38 of 1927)

Under the Bantu Administration Act, ministers and government officials have a right to prevent journalists from collecting news on developments in African areas. The State President is the Supreme Chief of African areas and can rule by proclamations. There have been 400 proclamations under which journalists have been arrested for writing on issues like political unrest, famine and poor living conditions. The Department of Bantu Administration has the right to decide what publications and films may be distributed in African areas. A journalist can get a permit to visit an African area only if the minister or government officials are convinced that he or she is unlikely to write articles or produce reports which are antagonistic to the policy of apartheid and its enforcement.

2 Suppression of Communism Act (no 44 of 1950)

Article 2 (B and D) defines "communism" as: (B) "(any doctrine or scheme).. . . which aims at bringing about any political, industrial, social or economic change within the Union by the promotion of disturbance or disorder, by unlawful acts or omission or by the threat of such acts or omissions or by means which include the promotion of disturbance or disorder, or such acts or omissions or threat; or (D) "which aims at the encouragement of feelings of hostility between the European and non-European races of the Union the consequences of which are calculated to further the achievement of any object referred to in paragraph (B)." This definition covers both communist and non-communist groups. The act is intended to protect the population from liberal and left-wing ideas. Any persons banned under the Suppression of Communism Act are prohibited from engaging in journalism; no publication is allowed to quote statements from a banned person. The State President has the right to ban any newspaper or publication which the government considers to be promoting any of the aims of communism or any ideas of persons or organisations banned under the act. There is no right of judicial appeal against government decisions taken under this act.

3 Public Safety Act (no 3 of 1953)

This act empowers the government to declare a state of emergency without recourse to parliament. Ministers then have unlimited powers to control or ban anyone, including the use of arrest and detention without trial, to close down newspapers, and suppress any news or dissemination of any material considered likely to incite people to oppose the government.

4 Criminal Law Amendment Act (no 8 of 1953)

Under this law it is a crime to advise, encourage or incite any person to protest against or campaign for the repeal of any law. This includes newspaper stories about planned protests. Bearing in mind laws like the Criminal Law Amendment Act, editors are compelled to exercise extreme self-censorship to avoid being charged. And generally, editors in the interests of their papers do exercise self-censorship.

5 Criminal Procedure and Evidence Act (no 56 of 1955)

Journalists must, to conform with this act, reveal their sources of information to a magistrate at the request of the public prosecutor. Failure to comply or to reply to any question renders one liable to imprisonment for up to one year.

6 Riotous Assemblies Act (no 17 of 1956)

This act makes it an offence to print, publish, advertise or make known any assembly which has been banned. It is a crime under section 2 (5) of the act to reproduce or disseminate in whole or in part "any speech, utterance, writing or statement made or produced . . . anywhere at any time by any person prohibited under sub-section 3 from attending any public gathering."

7 Official Secrets Act (no 16 of 1956) and the "Boss" Law (no 101 of 1969)

The Minister of Justice is empowered under this legislation to declare any area a "circumscribed" place within which nothing can be published and no photographs taken. It is an offence to publish any information relating to "any military, police or security matter"; "Security matter means any matter relating to the security of the republic and includes any matter dealt with by or relating to the Bureau for State Security (Boss). . . or relating to the relationship subsisting between any person and the said Bureau." (4) (Boss is the South African equivalent of the American CIA.) In five years of Boss's existence, its budget more than trebled, ie from R4 million in 1969—70 to R12.5 million in 1974—75. Responsibility for its activities rests with the Prime Minister and parliament is not entitled to know how Boss's money is spent. (5)

8 Post Office Act (no 44 of 1958), amended in 1972 and 1974

The Bureau of State Security is empowered to authorise the Post Office to intercept postal articles, telegrams and telephone messages and news reports. The Minister of Posts and Telegraphs, Mr F.C. Erasmus, told a party rally in November 1949 that "As Minister of Posts and Telegraphs I want to say to those people who send reports overseas slandering South Africa that they must not expect of me that all their reports will reach their destination. It is time the government put its foot down and it is doing so. (6)

9 Prisons Act (no 8 of 1959)

In order to prevent exposures of prison conditions, the government passed the Prisons Act. It is thus a crime to publish any information on prisons, prisoners and prison conditions which cannot be verified to the satisfaction of the law courts, or to take any photographs or to sketch any prison or prisoner without the written permission of the Commissioner of Prisons.

10 Extension of University Education Act (no 45 of 1959)

Under this act separate colleges were established for African, Coloured and Asian students. It restricts African students from producing magazines, newspapers or pamphlets without the permission of the rector; no statement may be made to the press by or on behalf of the students without the rector's assent.

11 Publications and Entertainments Act (no 26 of 1963)

Section 5 (2) of the act defines an "undesirable" publication as: "if it, or any part of it, is indecent, obscene, offensive, harmful to public morals, blasphemous, offensive to the religious convictions of any section of the inhabitants of the Republic, brings any section of the inhabitants into ridicule or contempt, is harmful to the relations between any sections of the inhabitants, or is prejudicial to the safety of the state, the general welfare, or peace and good order." The 1963 act was superseded by the Publications Act, 1974, which covers films, records, stage shows, artwork and inter alia, amateur photography; this empowers the government not only to ban current, but all future issues of a publication etc which might be considered "undesirable". There is no right of appeal. It is an offence to be found in possession of "undesirable" material even before it has been declared "undesirable".

12 Customs and Excise Act (no 91 of 1964)

Under this legislation any foreign publications or goods which are considered "indecent or obscene or on any ground whatsoever objectionable" by the Publications Control Board may be banned. The board, since its inception in 1963, had banned 20,000 publications by 1976; out of 1,208 publications submitted for scrutiny in 1973, 638 were found unacceptable.(7)

13 Defence Amendment Act (no 85 of 1967)

The Defence Amendment Act prohibits the publication of any information about military and naval activities without official approval. This Act made it impossible for communicators to write about various aspects of South Africa's involvement in the Angolan war in 1975. It is an offence to publish anything considered by the authorities to be capable of causing "alarm" or "depressing" the population. In many cases the only story which would not alarm or depress is that which supports the government's policies.

14 Newspaper and Imprint Registration Act (no 63 of 1971)

The act demands that the "intended nature and contents" and also addresses and former connections of the editors and personnel of all newspapers must be declared before registration and publication. For registration as a newspaper, a deposit of R10,000 to R20,000 is required if the Minister of Justice considers there is a possibility of the newspaper infringing the Suppression of Communism Act. In May 1971 all ten applicants for registration could not afford the deposit demanded and therefore were unable to launch their publications. The deposit is not refundable.

15 Provincial laws

The Provincial Councils of Transvaal, Natal and the Orange Free State have passed ordinances restricting the publication of material on grounds of indecency, offensiveness, profanity, and of being generally objectionable. With such laws in existence, it is impossible for there to be the sort of "freedom of the press" that it is sometimes claimed exists in South Africa. Under these laws aimed at protecting the status quo, journalists work daily under the threat of arrest and prosecution. They may communicate only certain information in a certain way approved by the authorities beforehand. It is illegal to interview certain categories of persons, especially those who have been banned. Journalists are like any other citizens in that they are not permitted to acquire banned or left-wing literature, even for research purposes. Like any other citizens, they are subject to all the laws of the racist society.

Distributors and censorship

Apart from the legal limitations on the freedom to receive and disseminate information, outlined above, further restrictions on the freedom of information are imposed by the existence of the Central News Agency (CNA) as the dominant distributor of the daily and weekly newspapers throughout the republic. As the biggest distributor of foreign newspapers, it is responsible for ensuring that none of these infringes in content any South African law. For instance, on May 9th 1963, quotations from a book by Ronald Segal, a banned South African, appeared in the British weekly, *The Listener*, and the CNA therefore had to delete the quotations to comply with the legal prohibition on quoting a banned person. In April 1968 the CNA deleted a letter from Walter Hain, a banned South African, from 8,000 coppies of the American magazine, *Life*. Since foreign editors naturally do not take South African laws into account when they publish material, such deletions are frequent occurrences.

News and newspaper distribution

The South African Press Association (SAPA) is a news agency, created by the main newspapers in 1938, whose service is limited to its members. The Argus group controls up to 87.4 per cent of the votes at a SAPA general meeting where the association's policies can be redefined. Under an agreement with Reuters, SAPA is in a monopoly position as regards the distribution of news in South Africa. CNA which enjoys a monopoly of newspaper distribution in the republic is like SAPA, it is owned jointly by the English and Afrikaans language newspapers. Its monopoly position militates against the creation of new publications and discriminates against some of those already in existence.

The police and the journalists

There has been conflict from time to time between the police trying to maintain "law and order" and journalists attempting to investigate some situation and publish those parts of their findings which would not be considered illegal by the state. In 1956 newsmen found themselves clashing with the police when they were trying to cover public demonstrations and protests against the treason trial then in progress. In 1957 the South African Society of Journalists sent a deputation to the Minister of Justice and the Commissioner of

Police over the question of police assaults on pressmen and destruction of films. The Commissioner in reply said that "pressmen among rioters must expect to be treated as rioters and that there was no reason for a newspaperman to be present during a riot as information could be obtained afterwards from a senior police officer."(8) As an attempt to clarify the relationship between the press and the police, an agreement was signed by the Commissioner of Police with the Newspaper Press Union in 1967, under which editors were obliged to inform the police before publication of any material concerning crime or "state security" which journalists might have obtained from sources other than the police. The police would consider whether the information should be printed or not. Certain privileges, like access to senior officers, were to be accorded to journalists possessing Press Identity Cards, which were themselves issued by the Police Commissioner.

Journalists continued to suffer harassment, arrests and banishments, especially those working for small publications which exposed injustice, discrimination and the worst aspects of apartheid. The number of people arrested or detained under the laws affecting the work of the mass media is so great that it would not be possible to list them in this book, nor indeed is it possible to obtain from the South African government a complete list of the victims and the details of their cases.

It is South African government strategy, instead of banning a newspaper — especially an internationally known one, to suppress the offending journal by arresting, banning and harassing its staff to a point where the paper is forced to practise self-censorship or go out of existence. The South African government is also keen not to damage continually its international image; this partly explains why the English language newspapers have been tolerated up to the present. The other reason is that these media do not in fact advocate fundamental changes to the present system, but campaign for social reforms which will help to bring non-Europeans into the economic life of the country for the betterment of the present economic system. The English papers are read by the majority of the white newspaper readers and to pressurise them more than has been done so far would escalate conflicts within the white community, which in turn would supplement the efforts of those who are trying to bring about fundamental political change in South Africa. The complex and loosely defined laws of South Africa have generally been applied more mildly to the English language papers and to other white liberal institutions and groups than to the black opposition.

The White Left and Black Papers

The ideological development of the African nationalist movement in South Africa was greatly accelerated by papers like *The Guardian,* a weekly controlled by the Communist Party of South Africa. *The Guardian* had a wider circulation among the black population than any other political paper of the time; the Malan Government banned it in 1952. But a week later, a similar paper was launched — the *Advance,* which was banned in 1954. Again, a week later, another, called the *New Age* and with a strong resemblance to its predecessors, was launched, much to the annoyance of the government. *New Age* was proscribed in 1962. A monthly, *Fighting Talk,* was banned in 1963. The *Workers' Unity, Spark, Contact* and *Clarion* have all either been banned or harassed out of existence.

Today what is called the Black Press is in fact white-owned and controlled. The best-known in this category is *The World.* But there have indeed been African-owned and run newspapers, as early as 1884 when Jo Tengo Jabavu started the *Imvo Zabantsundu.* In 1904 *Ilanga, Lase Natal* was launched by John Dube. *Izwi la Bantu* was begun by the Rev. Walter Rabusana, who later became Vice-President of the South African Native National Congress (SANNC) which in 1912 became the African National Congress (ANC). SANNC's official organ was *Abanthu Batho.* In Kimberley there was

Tsala ea Bat ho; Bloemfontein had the *Messenger Marumoa;* Pretoria the *Native Advocate.* Other papers which were short-lived were *Umlomo wa Bantu, African Shield,* and *Ikwezi le Africa.*

The Coloured and Indian organisations also published newspapers which were beset with the same financial problems as their African counterparts. They encountered the same hostility from the government too.

Some of the black-owned and run papers have articulated the aspirations of the black people of South Africa, serving as forums for debate on the black struggle for national liberation, and proving themselves useful means of mobilising the masses for many campaigns.

The Black and the Non-establishment Communicators and their Work

The political, economic and legal situation in Southern Africa makes the task of a black communicator extremely difficult and hazardous. It is not plain sailing either for his white counterpart, especially the one who is sympathetic to the freedom struggle or who is not consciously pro-establishment.

As is shown in this study, the political situation is oppressive, the legal system restrictive and the economic life of a black communicator shaky. A black communicator as a member of the black community suffers racial discrimination and other disabilities imposed by the state. He is not allowed into certain areas at all and some he can enter only at certain periods. The authorities do not permit him to report on some issues at all or in the way he might think fit. As an "opinion leader" in a community largely opposed to the political system of the country, he is automatically a man marked by the authorities.

A "non-political" writer, journalist, artist or any other communicator finds himself unconsciously conveying messages with political content. The style, presentation and pith, more often than not, reflect the sum total of a communicator's experience and that of his community. Also, politics permeate all facets of life in South Africa. In a portrait of the white South African short story writer and novelist, Nadine Gordimer, in *The Lively Arts* programme on BBC-2 television, London, on October 17, 1976, it was clearly shown how a seemingly "non-political" creative artist's work could easily be dismissed as political propaganda, or could lead to the artist's imprisonment.

One of Nadine Gordomer's short stories, *Something for the Time Being*, set in Johannesburg, shows the conflict between political principles and practice in two families, one white and the other black. The targets are the fake liberalism of the white family and the uncompromising militancy of the black one. The writer's original intention was not to produce a political short story, nor did she consciously think in terms of changing society when working on it. She was interested mainly in the human situations and individuals behind the facts and figures of the scene. But political doctrines played a dominant role and the characters were turned into representatives of those ideas more than anything else.

Her experience and that of her community entered automatically into her work as a communicator.

In 1975 local censorship committees were set up throughout the country. (9) All the 190 censors were white, with the exception of three Indians who vet Indian films and books. Most of the whites were Afrikaner-speaking Calvinists The only relaxation in censorship under the new system was reported to be on "nipples and buttocks." (9)   "Public morals, religion, the safety of the state", or anything which brings the white community and the socio-economic system into redicule or contempt, are considered to be the priority target for the censor's attention. Typical of the people chosen to be censors is the Rev. C. C. Colijn, a Dutch Reformed Church Dominee who declared: (9)   "Nudity belongs in the sacred confines of the bedroom of man and wife . . . Communism gratefully takes advantage of pornography to corrupt the morals, ethical concepts, and religious beliefs of a nation, making the takeover easy."

A book by an extremist Afrikaner which states that blacks "smell like stale biltong (dried meat) which is unfit for human consumption" and that "murder and robbery are inherent characteristics" of the African(9) was approved by the censors. But a play by an African which was highly commended by academics for its "literary merit" was proscribed because the censors thought it was "harmful to race relations". Anything violently antagonistic to black people is likely to be passed and anything opposed, even mildly, to white rule and oppression is likely to be banned.

South African black journalists have no choice but to identify with the aspirations of their community. An organization of black journalists, the Union of Black Journalists (UBJ), was formed as a nation-wide grouping. It held its third congress in Soweto on July 31 —August 1, 1976; 130 delegates from different parts of South Africa attended, including representatives of BPC and SASO. Speaker after speaker appealed for more commitment to the cause of african emancipation. Joe Thloloe, its president strongly appealed for unity and total identification with the struggle. The following clause was adopted and included in the preamble: "This closing of ranks is necessary for the realisation of the Black ideal — the creation of a non-racial society, in which the exploitation of man by man is completely eradicated". UBJ publishes *Bulletin of the UBJ*. Its aim is "... to disseminate information — the truth — to the oppressed and exploited masses".

Members of UBJ are prepared to take such a political line in spite of the hostility of the government and the usual arrests and harassment. A good number of officials and members like Joe Thloloe and Nat Serache have been detained several times and the latter who acted as a non-staff correspondent of the BBC World Service and made a name covering Soweto riots jumped bail and left the country after eleven successive days of savage torture by the Security Police. Many before them have also found themselves in prison, banishment or exile. But from inside or outside they will not be permanently silenced.

Though well known outside South Africa, many South African black writers in exile can only be read illegally inside their own country. They were gagged in the 50s and 60s under laws like the Suppression of Communism Act. Some of the most prominent among them are Ezekiel Mphahlele, Dennis Brutus, Lewis Nkosi, Mazizi Kunene, Bloke Modisane, and Alex La Guma. (10) A considerable number of whites also, like Ronald Segal, fall into the same category.

NOTES AND REFERENCES

1. See Benson, Ivor: *The Opinion Makers*, Dolphin Press, Pretoria, 1967, pages 91 and 92.
2. Rubin, Leslie: *Apartheid in Practice*, Unit on Apartheid, UN, New York, 1976, page 1.
3. These laws are listed in *Apartheid, Its Effects on Education, Science, Culture and Information*, Unesco, Paris, 1957, pages 185−203.
4. Quoted in Hepple, Alex: *Press Under Apartheid*, International Defence and Aid Fund, London, 1974, page 49.
5. See *Sunday Times*, Johannesburg, August 25, 1974.
6. Quoted in Hepple, Alex, op. cit., page 50.
7. *The Guardian*, London, August 23, 1976, and also *Rand Daily Mail*, Johannesburg, August 14, 1974.
8. Quoted in Hepple, Alex: op. cit., page 55.
9. Herbstein, Denis: "Verboten: the word that may isolate South African writers", an article in the *Guardian*, London, August 23, 1976.
10. See Notes and Documents No 2/75, *Books Banned in South Africa*, Unit on Apartheid, UN, New York, February 1975.

Chapter 3:
The Liberation Struggle

This chapter deals with the liberation struggle of South Africa as initiated, organised and led by black people of the area. Although there has always been a small number of whites who support the liberation struggle in South Africa, their role as a white left in a white racialist society has been complex and controversial. They are ostracised within their own community, easily identified by the authorities and suppressed. Their number, however, is bound to increase and their participation in the destruction of the white racist power structure will become more significant as the structure develops more cracks at the top and as it receives heavier and heavier blows from the bottom and elsewhere. The role of the white left, progressives and liberals demands a more detailed (and separate) treatment than is practicable here and so it falls outside the scope of the present study.

The history of the struggle for African liberation from white minority rule in South Africa is as old as the advent of the European settlers. As has been indicated, the coming of the Dutch, British and other Europeans to the area meant the immediate dispossession of the African's major means of livelihood, ie land and cattle, and also the denial of democratic rights. European colonialism in South Africa, as elsewhere in the world, meant that the indigenous people became second-class citizens. Colonialism brought segregation based on colour in every sphere of life in what many saw, and see, as a "great new visionary Christian civilisation".

All black people of whatever origin or orientation — from chief to servant, rich man to poor man, Christian to non-Christian, educated to illiterate, "tame" tribe to "hostile" — found they had a common oppressor who forced many of them to work for minimal wages. The role of an African in this society was to work for the achievement of maximum comfort for the white man at wages set sufficiently low just to allow the worker to return to his quarters each night, eat and report back in the morning, five to seven days a week, with no margin to allow him further freedom.

Up to the present time, the entire state machinery of South Africa is geared to systematically and perpetually safeguarding the social and material interests of the white ruling minority at the expense of the disenfranchised black majority. The primary function of parliament, the judicial system, the security forces and the socialisation agencies like the press is to maintain white power and keep the economy within white hands, to the total exclusion of the black people — except in so far as the blacks can be used in one way or another to uphold the status quo.

In pre-colonial days, the black people of South Africa were not one mass, under one government with one army. The Zulus, Xhosas, Tswanas, Sothos and others were independent nations, and like other nations elsewhere, had conflicting interests which led to wars from time to time. Hence, the early resistance against the European invaders was generally uncoordinated. The Africans fought separately as they were attacked or robbed of their land and cattle by the whites and at some periods they were made to take sides in inter-white military conflicts.

The technique of divide and rule was used not only among the different African nations, but also among chiefs of the same nation. For example, the Xhosa chiefs Ngquika and Ndlambe were incited to fight each other. Mpande of the Zulus was used against Dingane and, among the Sothos, Molapo was the instrument of betraying Langalibalele. Rivalries were also exacerbated among the Tswanas, the Kwena and the Kgaflea-Kyatle, the Tshidi-Rolong and the Ratlou-Rolong. Such divisions allowed the Europeans an earlier victory than might otherwise have been achieved. But, towards the end of the period, African solidarity was emerging. In the Lesotho "gun war" of 1880, for instance, when the Mpondomise, the Thembú and the Griqua people combined against the British Cape Colonists, the latter were defeated on that particular occasion. By an extensive use of messengers, key chiefs were beginning to coordinate their anti-colonialist struggle. But these moves came too late. The Africans were defeated in the military and political battles of that period.

Later, the major factors which brought about greater national contact and coordination among the black people, for the purpose of promoting their aspirations and defending their rights, were exploitation and racial segregation imposed by the whites, starvation, shortage of land, industrialisation, urbanisation and the existence of the modern information media, and literacy. Nation-wide African organisations were formed to carry on the struggle.

One such organisation, formed in 1912, is the African National Congress (ANC). The objectives set forth when the South African ANC was created were: (1)

"1. To unite all the various tribes in South Africa.
2. To educate public opinion on the aspirations of the black man of South Africa.
3. To be the mouthpiece of the people and their chiefs.
4. To advocate on behalf of the African masses equal rights and justice.
5. To represent them in the Union Parliament, and generally do all such things as are necessary for the progress and welfare of the African people."

Fruitless expeditions were made by delegations to the British government over some early manifestations of apartheid like the Land Act of 1913. Acts of civil disobedience, boycotts, strikes and other forms of non-violent passive resistance were organised. The more these protests and strikes occurred, the more repressive was the legislation brought into existence to protect the status quo.

On the industrial front, poor conditions, racial discrimination and meagre wages encouraged African workers to get organised. They found that they were being doubly oppressed, first as members of a conquered race and second as workers. The first and most important national organisation of black workers was the Industrial and Commercial Workers' Union (ICU), founded by Clements Kadalie, who was originally from Nyasaland (Malawi), in January 1919 in Cape Town; the first black workers' convention was held in Bloemfontein in 1920.

The ICU claimed a membership of 100,000 in 1926. It organised successful strikes and boycotts — its success being a sign of the ferment and discontent among the black population of South Africa. It had become both a trade union and a political organisation. Its structure was amorphous. The ICU encountered many problems in relation to the government. Many of its leaders and organisers were arrested or constantly harassed by the police. Opportunists and *agents provocateurs* were also to be found in the ICU membership and leadership. In the late 1930s the ICU was disintegrating as a result of internal and external contradictions and pressures. After the collapse of the ICU, many new trade unions serving separate industries and trades were established. The African labour movement remains an integral, and a major part of the liberation struggle.(2)

By the early 1930s the question of African participation in the decision-making processes of South Africa had become a most controversial and highly sensitive issue. It involved the whole subject of African versus white power. The government introduced three Native Bills (also known as the Hertzog Bills) which were meant to "settle the native question once and for all".(2)   The Bills led to the formation and consolidation of the All-African Convention (AAC) in 1935—37. The AAC was created as a result of conferences of about 112 organisations, with 500 delegates, aimed at promoting unity and resistance to the racial discrimination against the African people. The three Native Bills were passed in 1936 (Native Representation Bill, Native Trust and Land Bill) and 1937 (The Urban Areas Amendment Bill). Africans throughout the country felt deeply threatened by the Hertzog Bills, and it was during this period that the ANC and the ICU were found to be most wanting. They did not adequately mobilise the masses to face the new situation as people expected of them. Both organisations failed, at this most critical period of the African struggle, to provide the necessary leadership, and it was in this context that the AAC was born — as the result of a new and spontaneous movement for black national unity and militant activism. The AAC was intended to be a structure for African unity to which all organisations opposed to racist white minority domination would belong. As an organisation of organisations, its objectives were stated thus:(2)

(a) To act in unity in developing the political and economic power of the African people.

(b) To serve as the medium of expression of the united voice of the African people on all matters affecting their welfare.

(c) To formulate and give effect to a national programme for the advancement and protection of the interests of the African people.

(d) To assist in rehabilitating dormant and moribund African organisations and bringing together unorganised Africans into societies, communities or bodies affiliated to the All-African Convention."

Several officials of the AAC were also top executives of the ANC, but despite the overlapping membership, the two organisations were like rivals. Other organisations within the AAC were rivals and competitors. Petty sectarianism on the part of many constituent organisations of the AAC was another major destructive factor. But the idea of an All-

African Convention for unity and mass mobilisation marked an important stage in the development of the liberation struggle.

One of the important living offshoots of the AAC is the Unity Movement of South Africa, established in 1943 largely by the AAC, under the name Non-European Unity Movement. It was meant to follow the policy of total non-collaboration with the powers maintaining the status quo.

Another landmark in the struggle was a conference sponsored by the ANC and held on June 26–27th 1955, attended by Africans, Europeans, Coloureds and Indians, at Kliptown near Johannesburg. Three thousand delegates took part from the ANC, South African Indian Congress, South African Congress of Democrats, and the South African Congress of Trade Unions. This conference adopted the Freedom Charter (3) which declared: "South Africa belongs to all who live in it, black and white, and no government can justly claim authority unless it is based on the will of all the people... Our people have been robbed of their birthright to land, liberty and peace by a form of government founded on injustice and inequality... " The non-white demands in the Freedom Charter were set out thus:

"The people shall govern
All national groups shall have equal rights
The people shall share the country's wealth
The land shall be shared among those who work on it
All shall be equal before the law
All shall enjoy equal human rights
There shall be work and security
The doors of learning and culture shall be opened
There shall be houses, security and comfort
There shall be peace and friendship."

The very idea of black and white meeting to agree on such demands so greatly alarmed the government that police broke up the meeting on the second day, and a closer watch on the activities of the Congress followed. The Criminal Law Amendment Act (No 8 of 1953), which imposed heavy penalites like lashes, confiscation of property, fines and imprisonment for any form of resistance against apartheid laws (even non-violent resistance), was strengthened by the Native Administration Amendment Act (No 42 of 1956), which empowered the authorities to arrest and restrict Africans without trial, and Proclamation No 52 of 1958, which ensured strict control of the movement of Africans to and from the African homelands.

In a message to the white voters in April 1958, a few days before the elections, ex-Chief A.J. Luthuli, the then President of the African National Congress, declared: "We shall never rest content until the democratic principle which is conceded for Europeans is extended to include the entire population. Our aim is neither white supremacy nor black supremacy but a common South African multi-racial society, based upon friendship, equality of rights and mutual respect." (3)

The Pan-Africanist Congress of Azania (PAC) led by Mangaliso Sobukwe was formed in April 1959 mainly by members of the Youth League of the African National Congress who denounced the ANC for being dominated by white liberal forces and felt that it was no longer possible to use it as an effective machinery for militant action against the socio-economic system in South Africa. (1) PAC's aims included the following:

"to implement effectively the fundamental principle of the right to self-determination for African people;

to create an organisational machinery for the organisation and mobilisation of the African people into a powerful social force bent upon the destruction of all forces and factors that have reduced the stature of man and retarded his growth in our country, and to create conditions favourable for the restoration of man's human worth and dignity and for the full development of his social personality;

to work for the creation of a continental Union of African States as a concrete institutional form for the African nation;

77

and

we aim politically, at government of the Africans by the Africans for the Africans with everybody who owes his only loyalty to Africa, who is prepared to accept the democratic rule of an African majority, being regarded as an African. We guarantee no minority rights, because we think in terms of individuals and not of groups."

On race the PAC's position was stated as: (4) "The African people are very much proud of their race — the human race. They recognise no inescapable fundamental differences among members of even the three main branches of that race: Caucasoids, Mongoloids and Afrinoids. They regard the differences that exist among various groups or sub-groups of man to be mainly acquired in and through the individual factors in the acquisition of group characters. They do not, and will not, tolerate or foster sectional arrogance, and continued contempt for the worth of the human personality and disregard for human dignity."

By Proclamation No 119, April 8th 1960, the ANC and the PAC were proscribed and 11,279 Africans, 98 whites, 90 Indians and 36 Coloureds were arrested: 6,800 of the 11,279 Africans were arrested for breaking the pass laws. (5) In a speech at his trial in November 1962, Nelson Mandela, the leader of the African National Congress, said: (6) "Government violence can do only one thing and that is to breed counter-violence. . . if there is no dawning of sanity on the part of the government, the dispute between the government and my people will finish up by being settled in violence and by force. . . " Chief Gatsha Buthelezi, Chief Minister of Kwazulu, one of the Bantustans, also admitted in January 1975 that civil disobedience and economic disruption were inevitable if conditions of the non-white people did not change. His experience was that other means of effecting change in South Africa must be considered if it was not possible to reason with the white government. (7)

By 1960 the liberation organisations had become highly popular among the black population and increasingly effective in their campaigns and activities against the racist and inhuman system of government in South Africa. These actions took the form of strikes, boycotts, demonstrations and many different kinds of civil disobedience. The Defiance Campaign led by the ANC, which started in 1952, against the apartheid laws, and the anti-pass laws campaign, launched on March 21st, 1960 and led by the PAC, which resulted in the Sharpeville massacre, are some of the historic and well known courageous attempts by the liberation movement to win freedom and justice in South Africa. Since April 1960 the PAC, ANC and the Unity Movement have been forced to operate as underground movements in South Africa. From their external headquarters in Lusaka and Dar-es-Salaam they have tried to plan and organise guerrilla armies. Armed struggle is accepted as the main method of struggle. The independence of Mozambique and Angola is bound to facilitate armed struggle. The victories of the Vietnamese, Mozambicans, Angolans and Guineans through armed struggle have taught liberationists and their supporters in South Africa that guerrilla warfare fought inside a country and supported by the majority of the population, coupled by a favourable international climate, is bound to succeed, sooner or later. Bigotry and obstinacy on the part of the enemy and the continued existence of exploitation and oppression of the majority guarantee the success of guerrilla warfare. Organisations and leaders may come and go, but the struggle goes on and ultimately must succeed.

After arresting all the known leaders of the liberation movement in South Africa in 1960 in their thousands, during and after the events of April of that year, the government believed they had smashed the liberation struggle. They thought their task was then one of keeping the African population under close surveillance to prevent the emergence of new "agitators" and the resurgence of the struggle. But this proved to be another miscalculation typical of a reactionary ruling class. As long as oppression exists and people suffer its restraints, the struggle will continue. The only way to halt it is to eliminate the root cause of it — oppression, the germ of self-destruction carried by any system like the South African one. The mistake of the white ruling class is to confuse a particular liberation movement with the liberation struggle. Movements can disappear, but in time the continuing resistance to the stifling system produces new vehicles of defiance and struggle.

Apart from the ANC, PAC and Unity Movement, the struggle has thrown up new liberationist movements among the youth, the workers and the general oppressed population. The efforts of these later movements and of the older organisations, combined with the changed and now more favourable international situation, have resulted in the intensification of the struggle inside South Africa. This new stage has manifested itself in the appearance of the June 16th Movement, launched on that day in 1976 in Soweto, an African residential area in Johannesburg.

For several years after 1960 many activists decided to lie low or adopt the tactic of working within liberal organisations. They could not openly and on their own work for national liberation without being spotted, picked up and put away. This was a period of partly planned and partly spontaneous preparations for a new regroupment of the forces of liberation. It was a time of reflection on past mistakes making fresh analyses, identifying the strong and weak points of the enemy and unmasking its strategy and tactics. It was a period when individual activists were finding out who was thinking of and prepared to do what in their community, with a view to devising a common approach. It was at this time that the liberationists tested the possible reactions of the enemy to their future work.

South African Student Organisation (SASO)
After having made all these preparations for a regrouping of liberationist forces, eventually the South African Student Organisation was formed in December 1968 at a national conference of black student leaders. Many of SASO's top

activists had been working with the University Christian Movement (UCM), a white liberal dominated Christian organisation. SASO is concerned with drawing to the attention of the whole black population the nature of education operative in black universities. In connection with this, Ben Khoapa, Director of Black Community Programmes, wrote: (8) "Black students are increasingly resisting efforts to get them to cooperate in their own educational genocide. No longer can they be contained by white rhetoric; nor can they be seduced into rejecting the interests of their own people. They have learnt what a large number of black people are begining to learn from our young people, that revolution is not over and it is not just beginning, it's continually with us . . . "

The general aims of SASO as spelt out in its constitution are:

"to promote contact, practical cooperation, mutual understanding and unity among all black students in South Africa;

"to represent the interests of students on all issues that affect them in their academic and community situation;

"to heighten their sense of awareness and encourage them to become involved in the political, economic and social development of the black people;

"to project at all times the black consciousness image culturally, socially and educationally;

"to become a platform for expression of black opinion and represent these internationally."

SASO established projects in various parts of the country, namely: literacy campaigns; health projects, ie assisting in clinics and setting up new ones; physical projects, eg building schools and community centres; home education schemes, ie helping people trying to acquire higher education; black press project, concerned with publishing material on issues relevant to the problems and progress, or of interest to, the black community, increasing communication among the people and challenging and correcting distortions about the black community in the white establishment press; and leadership training programmes, ie teaching students efficient methods of running organisations.

The Black People's Convention (BPC)

The BPC was formally established at a conference held in Pietermaritzburg during 8—10 July 1972. The meeting was attended by 100 Africans, Coloureds and Indians. The BPC was preceded by several conferences organised around the concept of Black Consciousness, the first of which was held in April 1971. These gatherings had drawn delegates from more than 40 educational, welfare, religious, sport and youth organisations.

The BPC arose out of a conviction among leading members of various black organisations that, in spite of the attitude of the government and the likely consequences of its possible actions, black people must always have a nation-wide political organisation to promote and defend their political aspirations. If one body is banned, another must be formed immediately to replace it. The aims of BPC, according to the Conference report of July 1972, are:

to liberate and emancipate blacks from psychological and physical oppression;

to create a humanitarian society where justice is meted out equally to all;

to cooperate with existing agencies with the same ideals;

to re-orientate the theological system with a view of making religion relevant to the aspirations of the black people;

to formulate, apply and implement the principles and philosophies of Black Consciousness and Black Communalism.

The BPC opposes, and refuses to cooperate with the government and its institutions like Bantustans, the Coloured Peoples Representative Council and the South African Indian Council. The BPC decided to operate openly as a political party, with branches throughout the country.

The Black Allied Workers' Union (BAWU)

BAWU was established on August 27 1972, mainly through

the efforts of the Sales and Allied Workers' Association, which had been established in June, 1971. BAWU was started as an "umbrella trade union" which would cater for the interests of all black workers of South Africa. It includes the following in its aims: (9)

(1) "to organise and unite all black workers into a powerful labour force that would earn the respect and de facto recognition by both employers and government;

(2) to consult existing black trade unions;

(3) to effect the calling of a Black Workers' Conference, where the Black Workers' Council shall be elected;

(4) to improve the workers' knowledge through general and specialised (occupational) educational programmes, thus bettering workers' skills and know-how by conducting: (a) leadership courses, (b) labour seminars, (c) lectures and specialised commercial courses;

(5) to be spokesmen for black workers in any matters that affect them in the work field.

The Black Allied Workers' Union, the Black People's Convention and the South African Student Organisation overlap in their leadership, membership and aims. They also work closely together. They have been noticeably in the forefront of the African struggles which have culminated in the continuing workers' strikes and the struggles in Soweto and other parts of South Africa in 1975-7. Their work is complemented by the exiled movements. Sometimes there is direct and sometimes indirect coordination between the internally and the externally headquartered African groups and organisations for liberation.

These struggles quickly turned into a nationwide rebellion aimed at national liberation. From Soweto the struggle spread like wild-fire into Alexandra Township, Sebokeng, Atteridgeville, Garankuwa, Thembisa, Mamelodi, Kagiso, Natalspruit, Thokoza, Khotsong, Kwa Thema, Mlazi Witbank, Middleburg, Daveyton and Krugersdorp. The three black universities were forced to close, as was Qwaqwa seminary. Successful workers' strikes took place in Soweto, Port Elizabeth, Cape Town and other areas. White farms were burned, including that of H. Shoeman, Minister of Agriculture, whose farm in Transvaal suffered R100,000-worth of damage. Andre Kolver, Prime Minister Vorster's son-in-law, lost 2,000 sheep, apart from damage to land, buildings and other property in Orange Free State. (10) By December 1976 the nationwide black unrest was continuing unabated. It had reached every province of South Africa and its vibrations had disturbed the peace of every inhabited part of the country. If the level of the struggle was "successfully checked" by the authorities, as usual, it would in reality mean another temporary and tactical retreat which sooner or later would be followed by a resumption of the struggle at a higher and more intensified level than ever before. As long as the conditions which produce such a struggle exist, the movement for liberation cannot successfully and permanently be checked.

This Black revolt, which has been labelled as the "June 16th Movement", radically increased the contradictions within the centres of white power in South Africa. This is shown in the internal establishment debate of 1976 referred to in Chapter one.

BAWU, BPC, SASO and other allied organisations like the National Youth Organisation, the Southern African Students Movement (a high-school student organisation) and the Black Women's Federation have rapidly gained influence in the black community which has amazed the Vorster regime. It is these organisations which have collectively been called the "Black Consciousness Movement". Since the formation of SASO in 1968, the Black Consciousness Movement, ie the militant regeneration of the liberation struggle, has been felt in the white community. The blacks became increasingly uncontrollable and their consciousness against racism and political and cultural oppression reached a high and unignorable peak. The SASO view of Black Consciousness seems to be the operative definition among all the organisations

84

mentioned here. The SASO Policy Manifesto, approved by the Second General Students Council of July 1971, is reproduced in part here to show the definitions in it:

"SASO believes that:

3. (a) South Africa is a country in which both black and white live and shall continue to live together;
   (b) that the white man must be made aware one is either part of the solution or part of the problem;
   (c) that, in this context, because of the privileges accorded to them by legislation and because of their continual maintenance of an oppressive regime, whites have defined themselves as part of the problem;
   (d) that, therefore, we believe that in all matters relating to the struggle towards realising our aspirations, whites must be excluded;
   (e) that this attitude must not be interpreted by blacks to imply 'anti-whitism' but merely a more positive way of attaining a normal situation in South Africa;
   (f) that in pursuit of this direction, therefore, personal contact with whites, though it should not be legislated against, must be discouraged, especially where it tends to militate against the beliefs we hold dear.
4. (a) SASO upholds the concept of Black Consciousness and the drive towards black awareness as the most logical and significant means of ridding ourselves of the shackles that bind us to perpetual servitude.
   (b) SASO defines Black Consciousness as follows:
       (i) Black Consciousness is an attitude of

mind, a way of life.

(ii) The basic tenet of Black Consciousness is that the Black man must reject all value systems that seek to make him a foreigner in the country of his birth and reduce his basic human dignity.

(iii) The black man must build up his own value systems, see himself as self-defined and not defined by others.

(iv) The concept of Black Consciousness implies the awareness by the black people of the power they wield as a group, both economically and politically, and hence group cohesion and solidarity are important facets of Black Consciousness."

The liberation movement contains all people opposed in one way or another to white racist rule in South Africa. Workers, intellectuals, students, peasants, Christians, atheists, businessmen, chiefs, socialists, capitalists, moderates and militants, all can be members of, or any one of them could be a leader in the liberation struggle. The movements, the leaders and members may differ ideologically or on methods of struggle, emphasis or tactics, but can nevertheless belong to the same organisation in the interests of national unity among all racially oppressed people. The existence of a powerful common enemy produces national unity and encourages the strategy of different tendencies among the oppressed working together on the basis of supporting a minimum programme on which the maximum number can agree.

Although the elements spearheading the liberation struggle of South Africa do not always agree, they are united in their immediate objectives: the achievement of equal rights, and the elimination of racial segregation and exploitation of the black population by the white minority. The liberation movement as a whole is petty-bourgeois nationlist dominated. This dominant group is very similar to the aspiring bourgeoisie which is now in power in most of the ex-colonial states of Africa, Asia and Latin America where racist colonial administrations have been replaced with multi-racial capitalistic and indigenous-run regimes, which have a love-hate relationship with international imperialism.

The petty-bourgeois intellectuals and the indigenous businessmen who control these regimes immediately after national liberation has been achieved find that some of their former contradictions with imperialism have disappeared or are no longer that important. After independence imperialism to them is more like an ally than an enemy. They need its economic aid and other assistance to keep their regimes in power in the face of the masses of the people who expect a more meaningful national liberation. Before independence, some important elements in the leadership were opposed to the racist and exploitative system, not on principle but because it also victimised them personally and because that system was exlusively run by a racial minority of foreign origin. In other words, to put into their mouths a question which motivates their participation in the liberation struggle, they ask: "if the white upper classes of Europe are free from foreign interference and can exploit their own working classes, why can't we have the same freedom in the land of our ancestors to exploit our own lower classes?" They want a capitalist system which includes them or which does not discriminate against them. This element within the struggle, therefore, has a collaborationist outlook. It can easily compromise with the enemy because its contradictions with the enemy are not fundamental. It is ultimately for the same social order as the enemy defends. The contradictions which bother it can be solved without abolishing the entire system of capitalism.

Then there is the ever-growing socialist element in most of the liberation groups and organisations. It operates under the principle "unite with all those who can be united against the main enemy, and isolate your enemies one by one". The harder and the more protracted is the struggle for liberation, the stronger the socialist presence grows, eventually taking over the leadership of the movement. If the enemy regime is overthrown before the socialists are in control of the movement, then neo-colonialism results and the socialists are more likely to be purged from the new government, depending on the degree to which the new rulers are part of the international imperialist system.

Although today it is not possible, because of the way the country is run, to write about most aspects of South African politics without menitoning racial groups and conflicts based on colour and on ethnic backgrounds, in the final analysis the major national source of conflict is the way the country's wealth is distributed, and the growing gap between rich and poor. So, while initially the main conflict shows itself as a black versus white struggle, eventually, after the success of the present struggle, the conflict will more readily appear in its true and higher form and will then become more acute, more pressing and dominant than before. The main conflict then would be between those who use their economic and political power to enrich themselves at the expense of others, and thus put themselves in a position where they can control the lives of other people undemocratically, and those who are oppressed in the process. This eventual major conflict would not be based on race, but on class identification. It would be class struggle. Black liberation and independence under a capitalistic government will result in a new, higher struggle — class struggle. It is a higher form of struggle in that it vigorously aims at the abolition of classes. Its purpose is to create a classless and non-exploitative society. The whole state machinery after the true victory of socialist struggle will be geared to creating such a society.

If a new government assumed power in South Africa which was not based on colour or race, but was geared to creating a non-racial society, that would not in itself solve the problem of the re-allocation of national resources and wealth and ultimately eliminate the basis of class antagonism. A situation where there is a dominant minority, a rich multi-racial elitist ruling class and a poor, ruled and suppressed majority will

88

not prove a better proposition for the majority of citizens than the previous state of affairs. No one race of its nature has a monopoly of racist, selfish ideas. Given a certain historical background, ignorance, selfishness and opportunity, any group could oppress and exploit fellow human beings and formulate theories to justify its actions to itself, to the oppressed and to the outside world. After national liberation, the struggle continues, although national independence in itself is a step forward. It provides scope for the higher form of struggle – the class struggle, which seeks to eliminate the structured and state supported exploitation of man by man. It is part of a continuous process, with a number of complex stages within it.

NOTES AND REFERENCES

1. See chapter by Chimutengwende, Chenhamo: "Zimbabwe and White Ruled Africa", in *New Revolutionaries*, ed. Tariq Ali, Peter Owen, London, 1969. pages 241-244. Also see Tabata, I.B., *The Awakening of a People*, Bertrand Russell Peace Foundation, for Spokesman Books, Nottingham, England, 1974, pages 7 and 8.
2. Tabata, I.B., ibid.
3. Hepple, Alex: *South Africa, a Political and Economic History*, Pall Mall Press, London, 1966, pages 159-163.
4. See *Policy Programme of the PAC of Azania*, Pan Africanist Congress of Azania (SA), Dar-es-Salaam, 1972.
5. Hepple, Alex: op cit, page 165.
6. Quoted in Hepple, Alex: ibid, page 164.
7. See "Vorster Pledges of Reform Disappoint Black Leaders", *The Times*, London, January 25, 1975.
8. See Khoana, B.A., ed., *Black Review 1972*, Black Community Programmes, SASO, Durban, 1973, page 22.
9. Khoapa, B.A., Ed.: ibid, pages 41-2.
10. For details of the struggle in South Africa from June 16 to December 1976 see
    (a) *Focus*, news bulletin of the International Defence and Aid Fund, London (issues of the period concerned);
    (b) *Azania Combat*, PAC of Azania (South Africa) Observer Mission to the UN, New York (issues of the period concerned);
    (c) *Sechaba*, ANC of South Africa, London (issues of the period concerned);
    (d) *The African Nationalist*, ANC of South Africa (African Nationalists), Dar-es-Salaam (issues of the period concerned);
    (e) *Soweto, June 1976, The Call to Arms* by V.K. Scrpae Ntshona of the Unity Movement of South Africa (extracts of which appear as an appendix to this book).

Chapter 4:
Information Work: the State versus the Liberation Movement

South African Government Propaganda
On 26th January, 1976, Mr P.W. Botha, the South African Minister of Defence, stated: 'Today we are being regarded in a different light in Africa. A large part of Africa is recognising to an ever-increasing extent, that South Africa may be relied upon as an African state' (House of Assembly Debates, Hansard, 26—1 -76).

Dr C.P. Mulder, the Minister of Information, emphasised South Africa's attitude to independent Africa when, on 18th October, 1974, he urged: "South Africa must have more frequent contact with the rest of Africa as soon as possible. After all that's where the key lies. If we can convince Africa of our integrity, we will then be more readily accepted by the rest of the world . . . The challenge is to convince the bulk of the Black African states that the divisions should not be Black—White but Communist and anti-Communist" (quoted in *Sechaba* ANC, Dar-es-Salaam, March, 1975).

Dr Mulder showed his department's determination and strategy when he explained: "My department will not remain on the defensive. We have now gone over to the offensive. We are now equipped with an area map, so to speak, on which we can intelligently base our strategy — a map which shows up enemy strength and weakness and their respective positions" (South African Parliamentary debate, 2nd October, 1974).

The foregoing quotations clearly show the propaganda strategy and resolve of the South African government.

In 1975 the budget of the Information Department was £6,562,500. This was only £1,875,000 less than that allocated to the Department of Foreign Affairs. The underlying aim is to influence the thinking of the population of South Africa as a whole, with the secondary target being the hostile international opinion.

By having so many laws regulating the press, South Africa ensures that the information which gets to its populace supports the principle of white rule — or at least is not violently and fundamentally opposed to it. International acceptability, especially in Africa and the Western world, is also a special priority in the South African propaganda offensive. The aim of the "information" offensive is to induce the world to accept South Africa as "an independent African state where black and white live separately as they wish and peacefully". Having realised that apartheid is an unacceptable policy, internationally, South Africa has tried several times to change the name of the policy without altering the content of it. In South Africa "information" publications apartheid has been called "parallel development", "separate development", or "separate freedoms". "Baaskap", an Afrikaans term meaning white rule, was replaced by "buurskap", which translates as "neighbourliness". The policy of arbitrarily dividing Africans into eight tribal groups has been termed "self-determination of African nations", while all white people are united irrespective of their diverse national origins. Sometimes this old colonialist technique of divide and rule is dignified with the title "multi-nationalism".

As reported in *The Times,* London, September 15, 1976 Dr Connie Mulder told the Transval Congress of the National Party in Pretoria on September 14, 1976, that "apartheid" and "separate development" had negative connotations abroad. Apartheid was interpreted by enemies of South Africa, especially those overseas, as "aparthate", and where "separate development" was used, the emphasis was put on "separate". Dr Mulder therefore declared that "plural democracy" should replace the old terminology because it was an acceptable international term. But like Mr Vorster, Dr. Mulder said that he was thinking of overhauling the terminology only as a propaganda measure and not of reversing government policies which have been vigorously pursued since 1948.

When the United Nations Security Council was considering the expulsion of South Africa in October 1974, the South African government produced a new propaganda line to the effect that it was going to remove "unnecessary discrimination", and this was the reason given by France, the United Kingdom and the United States for using their vetoes to defeat the resolution to expel South Africa. South Africa's chief delegate to the UN, to the surprise of all, said: "Discrimination based solely on the colour of a man's skin cannot be defended, and we shall do everything in our power to move away from discrimination based on race and colour."(1) Thanking Britain, France and the US for having used the veto in South Africa's favour, Mr Vorster said, on 5 November 1974:(2) "There were matters which could not be made public at this stage", but added, "All I ask . . . is to give South Africa a chance of about six months. I do not ask more than that. If South Africa was given that chance the commentators would be surprised at the country's position in six to 12 months' time."

Two years later, however, racial discrimination remains intact and enforced by law. On 23rd April 1976, the *Financial Mail* commented: "not one of the 87 bills presented to parliament so far this session reflects government's professed commitment to move away from racial discrimination". Only one theatre, the Nico Malan Theatre in Cape Town, was opened to audiences of different races. "Whites Only" notices were removed in very few places, while 20 hotels and one restaurant were granted "international status" in February 1976. But restrictions were also imposed as follows:(3)

(1) no more than 15% of the hotel beds can be taken by Blacks at any one time;

(2) South African Blacks may not be admitted to men's bars or allowed to take part in dancing; and

(3) the use of any swimming pool on the premises must be restricted to *bona fide* guests who are resident in the hotel.

Another propaganda line has it that South Africa is a bastion against "communism" in Africa and that, with its control of the Cape sea route, it is an essential ally of the West — especially since 1967 when the Suez Canal was closed. However, the growing international opposition to apartheid makes it difficult for the Western countries to publicly accept South Africa as an ally. South Africa could have done well as far as open acceptability went among its allies only if the "cold war" had been at its height. Even on Angola, the Western nations could not militarily come to the aid of South Africa. South Africa had invaded Angola under the pretext of fighting against communism and keeping the area within the western sphere of influence. South Africa overestimated its own military power and miscalculated in that it failed to appreciate that America or any western country would think twice before sending its troops to a country where a possible Vietnam-like situation could develop.

While opposing a relaxation of international tensions, South Africa desperately wants *detente* in Africa, ie between itself and the Black African states which materially and morally support the liberation movements of South Africa. But *detente* in this sense means African states abandoning their commitment to those liberation movements. Consequently only a few tractable African states have responded favourably to South Africa's *detente* overtures.

Up to the early 60s South Africa was opposed to the granting of independence to African territories, and used to refer to these countries in highly insulting terms. Then when it realised that African independence was a reality, it sought to establish relations with the previous untouchables, offering "aid and non-aggression pacts". It realised that unless it could be accepted by African states, the western world, with its economic stake in Africa, would not easily accept South Africa either. With the success of the Mozambique and Angolan liberation struggles, the progress of the Zimbabwe freedom fighters and the resistance against racist power inside South Africa itself, South Africa calculated that if it cooperated with African states in settling the Rhodesian issue, it would thereby achieve greater acceptability. It realised that Rhodesia was the next to go and that the best it could do was to control and direct the change and thereby establish a pro-West neo-colonial state. Such a state would not easily be used as an external base by South African freedom fighters. It would serve as a buffer zone rather than be a militant African state committed to the liberation of South Africa. South Africa saw that the most likely outcome if the white minority government was defeated militarily would be a militant and progressive Zimbabwe. This line of reasoning, however, underestimates the power of Zimbabwe people to defeat neo-colonialism and the capacity of the people of South Africa to fight for their own liberation.

Meaningful and lasting co-existence or *detente* with African states has proved impossible because of the fact that Africans within South Africa itself are still oppressed and racially discriminated against. Were any African state to attempt to cooperate with South Africa, it would find that public opinion at home was bitterly opposed to such a move. It is necessary here to give a brief account of the background to the South African-Western sponsored *detente* exercise which reached a turning point in 1974/5.

Enjoying the support of South Africa and Portugal, prior to the Portuguese coup of 1974, the Rhodesian government had not been desperately worried about guerrilla warfare, although by early 1974 the Rhodesian guerrilla movement was becoming stronger and stronger and Rhodesia was beginning to feel the pinch.(4) As for South Africa, Rhodesia was a useful buffer zone against South African guerrillas coming from Zambia and East Africa. It made military sense for South Africa to fight South African guerrillas hundreds of miles from her own border. South Africa therefore sent 2,000 –4,000 military personnel to help the Rhodesian forces after the Rhodesian declaration of independence.

South Africa and Portugal too had always thought that because of their interests the NATO countries of Europe and North America would come to the assistance of white ruled Africa if it was threatened by African guerrillas who were militarily supported by Russia and China. These interests are economic and political. US and western policy towards South Africa was aimed at protecting those interests. It was a policy "based on the premise that blacks cannot gain political rights through violence. . . The whites are here to stay and the only way that constructive change can come about is through them. . . violence would only lead to chaos and increased opportunities for communists." (5)

The racial nature of the conflict and the need to maintain influence among members of the Organization of African Unity made it difficult for the US to align itself publicly with the white minority regimes and the Portuguese colonial policy in Africa. So the US tried to keep a low profile in the area for a while.

The the coup d'etat in Portugal on 25 April 1974, which meant that Angola and Mozambique became independent under the guerrilla movements of the areas changed the whole political picture in Southern Africa.

The effects of the Portuguese colonial wars on the contradictions within metropolitan Portugal had been underestimated, especially by the "Vorster, Smith and Caetano alliance". Portugal had been involved in 14 years of colonial wars which were absorbing half of Portugal's state budget annually. Inflation; mass emigration of young workers, peasants and technicians; the desertion of soldiers from the army; the growing number of people, especially the young, killed or handicapped; all these connected with the war in

96

Africa escalated the contradictions in Portugal itself. (6) The war in Africa helped to produce a left-wing government in Portugal which was determined to give independence to the African colonies under the leadership of the guerrilla movements. This meant that Rhodesia could no longer defend its borders against guerrillas, since from Mozambique's independence on 25 June 1975, Rhodesia was to share nine-tenths of her borders with independent African states: Zambia to the north, Botswana to the west, and Mozambique to the east.

As members of the OAU, Rhodesia's neighbours would be duty-bound to help Rhodesian guerrillas and to implement UN economic sanctions. Mozambique's sea ports were to be closed to Rhodesian goods and South African ports and the railway links with Rhodesia were not expected to be capable of handling all Rhodesian goods.

South West Africa was to have a long border with an independent African state, Angola, from 1 November 1975. This meant that South West African guerrillas would pass in and out of South West Africa more or less freely. In fact, a few months after the Lisbon coup d'etat, more than 2,000 mostly young Africans fled South West Africa through Angola for guerrilla training in independent Africa. (7) About 20,000 young Zimbabweans were also able to leave Rhodesia for Mozambique and Zambia seeking military training in order to be guerrilla fighters. General William Yarborough, (8) the former head of the United States Special Forces and US security consultant, in early 1974 came to Rhodesia's northeast province where most of the guerrilla warfare was taking place. The purpose of the visit was to advise on the defence of "strategic villages." Yarborough's observation was: "Southern Africa had the makings of another Vietnam". The Rhodesian security forces, making their own observations, had also told Ian Smith that "the war against the guerrillas was, in the long run, militarily unwinnable." (8) Before the Lisbon coup d'etat, the Rhodesian guerrilla movement, far from being on the decline, was growing as increasing

areas bordering Rhodesia were coming under the control of
FRELIMO guerrillas, who were assisting Zimbabwe freedom
fighters with bases nearer their target areas inside Rhodesia.(9)
With FRELIMO's coming to power in Mozambique, Rhodesia
was no longer going to remain a "buffer zone" for South
Africa. The leader of South Africa's white trade unions,
Mr Arthur Grobbelaer, when invited to address the Rhodesian
Trade Union Congress, said: "It is realistic to recognise that
while your country has until now acted as a buffer zone in
blunting terrorist incursions from black Africa, your importance to South Africa for that purpose has now declined." (10)
The Zambezi River was no longer the dividing line between
white-ruled Africa and the independent African states. On
29 September 1974, South Africa's Prime Minister Mr Vorster
visited Ivory Coast to meet some representatives of certain
OAU member states to seek support for his Bantustan policy
and also to offer to help pressurise Rhodesia's white minority
to settle with the Rhodesian African nationalists. (11)

In October 1975, Donald B. Easun, US Assistant Secretary
for African Affairs, was in Lusaka organising a conference of
US Ambassadors in Southern and Central Africa which took
place early in November and at which US policy in Africa
was reviewed. When he returned to the US, he told Congress:
"I do not honestly see how one can look at the situation in
South Africa and feel that change is not going to occur."(11)
US policy was now aimed at winning Mozambique away from
the Soviet and Chinese influence, and peaceful change in
Southern Africa was seen as conducive to the establishment
and maintenance of US influence in the area.(11)

On 23 October 1974, Mr Vorster, inter alia, made the
following points: (12)

(a)   that South Africa was ready to work for a peaceful
      settlement of the South African situation;

(b)   that South Africa was anxious to see peace in Rhodesia;

(c)   South Africa appealed to those with influence over
      Rhodesia to use it for peaceful change.

Three days later, President Kaunda of Zambia(12) referred to Vorster's speech as the "voice of reason" which Africa had been waiting for. The speech was followed by official contact between Zambia, acting on its own and on behalf of some African states, and South Africa which had indicated that it would help on the Rhodesian issue. The African states concerned were basing their actions on the OAU Lusaka manifesto.(1 3)

The South African government was willing to cooperate (14) with the OAU on Rhodesia and South West Africa, but there were problems on either issue. Over South West Africa, South Africa was not willing to negotiate with SWAPO, which the OAU and the UN Council for Namibia recognise as the main liberation movement; and South Africa wanted "self-determination" for South West Africa based on its apartheid and Bantustan policies, which is unacceptable to the other side. On Rhodesia, South Africa was willing to "force" the Smith government to settle with Africans on the basis of African majority rule; the problem up to September 1977 was how far Vorster's government could "pressurise" or "force" Smith's government to settle peacefully with the Africans, without provoking an uncontrollable and disastrous right-wing back-lash in South Africa itself.(1 5) Even if South Africa succeeded in engineering the resolution of the Rhodesian and South West African conflicts to the satisfaction of the OAU and UN, there would be still no real *detente* and dialogue with it unless changes took place in South Africa itself soon enough and to the satisfaction of the international community and the South African liberation movements. Most African states would not find it possible politically to establish diplomatic, trade and other economic links with South Africa as long as apartheid remained in force; and *detente* and dialogue without such links would fall far short of South Africa's original aspirations.

Mr Vorster, in Cape Town on 20 February 1975, clarified his position on the issue when he said that (16) "he had dedicated himself to normalising relations between his country and the rest of the continent. His government would do everything possible to bring about peace, particularly in Southern Africa, but at the same time had no intention of dropping its policy of apartheid."

South Africa's official propaganda cannot be effective, therefore, because of the fascistic and obnoxious nature of apartheid — which is the sole cause of the present international isolation of South Africa. As a South African opposition member of parliament put it: "It is high time we realised that apartheid is a non-saleable commodity anywhere in the world. Until we accept this fact, we may as well try to sell ice cream in the Antarctic." (17)

The South African government, while being aware of the international hostility to apartheid, remains obstinately determined to defend its indefensible policies. Apart from publishing scores of "information" documents like the *South African Digest* and *Panorama*, distributed by the South African embassies, the Information Department has indirect methods of disseminating propaganda. These are:(a) financing pro-South African magazines and papers; (b) advertising speeches by Bantustan leaders like Chiefs Mangope and Matanzima appealing for economic aid for their Bantustans and against the economic boycott of South Africa; (c) advertisements attacking and ridiculing critics of South Africa; and (d) appointing black Information Officers in embassies serving countries where there is considerable opposition to apartheid. The Secretary of the Department of Information, Dr Eschel Rhoodie, on 10 October 1972, said that the aim of the Department was that 50–60% of its work should be indirect propaganda.

Prominent among organisations making propaganda for South Africa is the South African Foundation, which was formed after the Sharpeville massacre for the purpose of projecting the "correct image of South Africa". The Foundation supports apartheid indirectly by opposing any boycotts or campaigns or action against South Africa. It is financed by business companies and has offices in London, Bonn, Paris and Washington, and has pro-South African propaganda committees in Austria, Australia, Belgium, Canada, Denmark, Finland, France, West Germany, Greece, Israel, Italy, Lebanon, Holland, New Zealand, Norway, Portugal and Switzerland. The South African press is well represented on the Board of Trustees of the Foundation; in 1960 when it was established, the following were among its members: (18) Anton Rupert, Director of *Dagbreek;* A. Bearild, Chairman of CNA Ltd and Director of the Bantu News Agency; Clive S. Corder, Director, *Cape Times,* Barclays, Union Castle, Goodyear Tyres, Schweppes, Syfrets Trust; G.H.R. Edmunds, Chairman of SAAN, Deputy Chairman of the South African Board of the Standard Bank of South Africa, Director of several mining companies, Chairman of the *Rand Daily Mail* and the *Sunday Times* syndicate; Dr A.L. Geyer, Director of *Nasionale Pers,* and former editor-in-chief of all its publications, chairman of SABRA, Director of Barclays DCO, English Electric, former editor of *Die Burger,* former High Commissioner in London; Dr P.J. Meyer, political correspondent of *Dagbreek,* later Chairman of the South African Broadcasting Corporation; Dr M.S. Louw, Director of *Dagbreek;* Dr F.H. Du Toit, Alternative Director of Dagbreek Trust. Although some of these people have ceased to be Trustees of the South African Foundation, through retirement, old age or whatever, their places have been taken by people of equivalent rank and influence in South African press and business circles. In 1975 the Foundation admitted influential, but of course pliant, blacks to its membership. (19)

The South African Foreign Policy Association, formed in 1975 by businessmen, is another propaganda institution whose importance and work for South Africa has greatly increased during its brief life. In April 1976 the Association organised a well-publicised three-day international symposium in the capital of the Bantustan of Transkei. Influential rightwing academics and businessmen and pro-South African lobbyists from Britain, the United States of America, Israel,

Taiwan, West Germany and France attended the symposium. The participants were in the main people having connections with racist and "cold war" groups and trade associations which advocate continued economic and cultural links with South Africa. They have access to the press and contacts in high government and business circles in western countries. The Association aims at giving the necessary intellectual backing to South Africa's propaganda activities.

South West Africa

The dominant political aspirations of the whites in South West Africa and Rhodesia are essentially the same as those of South African whites. The three countries together form the last stronghold of European colonialism and imperialism in Africa. The European populations of these countries co-operate in almost every sphere of life and South Africa acts as big brother. Most Europeans in Rhodesia and South West Africa regard South Africa as their main power base politically, militarily and economically. Without South Africa's support they would have had to succumb to the forces of African liberation much earlier. In turn, South Africa's power base is the western powers.

The UN-mandate territory of South West Africa is a mere extension of the Republic of South Africa in almost every respect, being ruled by South Africa as one of its provinces — a subject of dispute between South Africa and the United Nations. There are four establishment daily newspapers in South West Africa: the *Suid Wester,* an Afrikaans mouthpiece of Vorster's ruling Nationalist Party; *Suid West Afriakaner,* which supports the United Party of South Africa and the creation of Bantustans; the neo-fascist German language paper, *Allgemeine Zeitung,* which adheres to the ideology of Hitler's Germany; and the *Windhoek Advertiser,* an English liberal daily. In 1969 a bantustan-oriented radio network was established by the South African government with regional "tribal" stations in Ovambo, Nama, Herero, Kavango, etc. The broadcasts are full of the glories of the South African government's philosophy of bantustans and reasons why the Africans should not opt for any other solution to their problems.(20)

Rhodesia

Rhodesia has similar laws to those of South Africa. For instance, one of the most often invoked laws in Rhodesia against the media is the Law and Order (Maintenance) Act, 1960, which, inter alia, states that "any person who. . . causes to be printed any subversive statement shall be guilty of an offence. . . (21) A subversive statement is defined as "any statement which is likely. . . to excite disaffection against. . . the government or constitution of Rhodesia by established law. . . "(21)   Even church-owned newspapers, bu read mostly by Africans, like *Moto,* have been among those banned under this legislation, or constantly harassed like *Umbowo.*

All the establishment newspapers of Rhodesia, like the *Rhodesia Herald* and the *Bulawayo Chronicle,* are not only subject to censorship and control of what is published, but also have private arrangements with the government not to print anything embarrassing or hostile to the authorities. (21) But, in spite of the self-censorship and press collaboration with the state, journalists continue to be arrested even for writing embarrassingly pro-government statements: the laws are so confused and loose that many pro-government journalists are not likely to know for certain whether they are supporting the government in the correct way. The question of what is expected of them by the government can be a thorny one for newsmen. Government attitudes and policies are highly unpredictable.

For external propaganda, the Rhodesian government has depended mostly on South Africa. Rhodesia, because of the illegal nature of the Smith regime, has no diplomatic mission in any part of the world except South Africa. To make propaganda for South Africa is to make propaganda indirectly for Rhodesia. Like South Africa, Rhodesia cannot join the Organization of African Unity because of its racist and old-style colonial outlook. But, unlike South Africa and in terms of international law, Rhodesia is not legally independent and therefore not a member of the United Nations Organization. It also lacks resources to mount international propaganda through right-wing fascist groups and other independent channels. Internally, apart from the main newspapers and the Rhodesia Television, the other important medium for Rhodesian government internal propaganda is the African Service of the Rhodesian Broadcasting Corporation. The main items in the African Service are quizzes, music, anti-African nationalist gossip and innuendoes, education and news programmes. (22)

There is a daily programme called *Padare*, which is a discussion by three or four people before the news. It deals with developments inside and outside Rhodesia, the aim of the programme being to discredit African liberation movements and support the Rhodesian government in the most plausible way possible. Some of the main items for discussion are distorted and exaggerated accounts of upheavals in African states and the imaginery evils of communism, and these are alluded to in such a way as to make them inseparable from the objectives and activities of liberation movements.

The African Times, a 16-page fortnightly, beautifully printed by offset litho, with a circulation of 325,000 (1970), is another important means of disseminating government propaganda among the Africans. It is distributed, free, to all schools, missions and other establishments where Africans are to be found in big numbers. Its aim is to supplement other government propaganda efforts. Its tactics are the same as *Padare's*: attacking liberation movements; promoting government development principles and programmes; showing the skill, dedication and power of the government forces; and promoting African chiefs. (22)

But the whole propaganda strategy and style underestimates the intelligence of the African people. The assumption underlying it is that you can oppress a people, racially discriminate against them and virtually turn them into slaves, then assure them that they could never be happy in any other situation, and that if they are hungry they should not ask for food because it is not good for them — only for white people – and at the end of it all expect them to believe this palpable absurdity and remain passive. The effectiveness of political propaganda is not based merely on its volume and on how beautiful the appearance of the media is. The content of the propaganda and its relevance to the aspirations of the audience are the factors of paramount importance. The information must point out ways through which the hungry can escape from their situation as quickly as possible. It must explain how discrimination and oppression can be ended, or else that propaganda will not be successful. In fact, more often than not, when propaganda misfires, it is counterproductive.

One thing about government propaganda in South Africa, South West Africa and Rhodesia is that it helps the thinking Africans, the activists and the patriots to understand better the mind of the enemy, his strategy and tactics, and his weaknesses. Any concessions by the enemy are revealed through his information media. Concessions made by the oppressor to the oppressed are signs of defeat and therefore a source of inspiration to the oppressed to maintain and even increase the level of fighting. By making concessions, the enemy may be trying to turn defeat into victory for himself, or trying to coopt and neutralise the struggle. Government propaganda in such a situation therefore can be used by the revolutionaries to sustain a high degree of vigilance and to raise the morale of the people through constant counter-information work among them; exposing various myths about the invincibility of white minority rule and its machinations against the oppressed. Its propaganda can be studied, analysed and exposed to the people by the liberation movement.

Information Work and the Liberation Movement

The African movements and groups organising resistance against oppression are faced with tremendous South African internal and external propaganda, which is well financed and coordinated under an experienced government department with an elaborate network and almost unlimited facilities. The issue of information work therefore confronts every organisation or movement engaged in spearheading, or which is concerned with, the struggle or war of national liberation. A liberation movement finds itself faced with the tasks of counteracting enemy or hostile propaganda; correcting distortions and malicious speculations; and maintaining the right image of its aims and membership — in fact, more than this, it must be on the offensive. Different organs of the movement have to remain in constant contact with each other; for the movement to recruit and grow, it must fully understand, and be fully understood by the masses of the people; information must flow to and from the movement. Apart from inter-personal channels of communication, the media of mass communication are used, and must be used, to the maximum level.

The mass media in Southern Africa are, as we have seen, owned and controlled by pro-government interests, by the government itself, or by economic interests opposed to African liberation as defined by African liberation movements. The mass media must be thus aligned by virtue of their ownership and control, and in order for them to be allowed to exist legally for a long time. The pattern of ownership and control of the mass media in South Africa, Rhodesia and South West Africa is owned by the same economic and commercial interests which control their South

African counterpart. It follows that the use of the mass media by the liberation movements in Southern Africa is usually nil, and in certain periods minimal. The media are therefore not on the side of African liberation. But because of certain contradictions within the white community, the unjust nature of white minority governments and the inherent seeds of self-destruction in the racist system in Southern Africa, it is possible — only occasionally, but not insignificantly — for the opposition movement to use the mass media.

In fact, since the media are the leading barometer of the levels of contradictions within the ruling class, some of the media represent the interests of the enlightened sections of the establishment. The distinction between the most enlightened sections of the ruling class and the most liberal sections of the opposition movement is sometimes extremely fine and there is occasional fraternisation. It is often through this hobnobbing that opposition information filters into the ruling-class media. Apart from that, a ruling class group, in an effort to score a point against the other sections of society, may publish information and news in its media about the revolution and the views of its leaders. Journalists also are in a dilemma: as has been argued earlier, they have a duty to inform the ruling class about all developments and events affecting the security and interests of the state. But to report accurately and meaningfully, they must publish material especially on the problems and progress of the liberation struggle for the establishment, and by so doing, they render indirect service to the forces of liberation. The media are disseminating information from the movement to its constituency and potential supporters — which is what the movement wants. From time to time liberationists and their sympathisers are asked by reporters to state their views on certain current events and issues and they always seize such opportunities to express their opinions even if their statements are not reported in full. Letters to the editors favourable to the ideas of the liberation movements sometimes do get printed. Opposition activists undertake special campaigns of writing letters for publication aimed at demystifying the concept of the invincibility of white rule and exposing various aspects and activities of the racist state.

A true liberation movement automatically finds that it must disseminate its ideas among the people from whom it seeks support, sympathy and recruits, all without which it would fail in its mission. The ideas and principles of a liberation movement can be communicated to the people through public rallies, small discussion groups and person-to-person discussions — all of which are strengthened or fed by broadcasts and the printed media of communication at the disposal of the liberation movement. Any liberation movement which ignores the importance of machinery for spreading information among the people, whose struggle it is supposed to be the vanguard of, and among the international community could well find that credit for its work is attributed to fake movements, or the enemy simply and successfully suppresses reports on the progress of the struggle.

A constant flow of information from the liberation movement to the people not only helps the movement to win more recruits, cadres and supporters, it also helps to maintain high morale among its supporters who may easily become victims of enemy propaganda. The flow of information from the masses of the people to the movement's leadership and activists helps to maintain intact the integration of the leadership and activists with the people, which is an essential aspect of any true revolutionary process. Every liberation movement, therefore, needs a strong propaganda and information machinery to facilitate this revolutionary and educational process among the people. In fact, the existence of such machinery is a sign of foresight, maturity and sophistication on the part of a liberation movement. It is a sign of its being a people's movement and is an integral part of its development. Any liberation struggle which does not involve the masses of the people becomes an elitist struggle which (if it succeeds) is bound to replace one set of exploiters with another. No revolution is likely to succeed without the mass involvement of the people, and if such a struggle managed at all to topple the enemy, it would not succeed in consolidating the victory without the full participation of the people. In any case, revolution is not merely the act of overthrowing a regime but also a matter of liberating man's mind, attitudes and way of life. Indeed, it is a permanently continuous educational process.

In certain periods of the national struggle the liberation movements have been allowed by the regimes of South Africa, Rhodesia and South West Africa to communicate with the populace, its supporters, cadres and sympathisers through public meetings and group discussions. When this "freedom" of assembly and information has been allowed under the watchful eye of the security forces, the liberation movements have found it important to use the newspapers, magazines and radio whenever possible. The movements also publish their own newspapers, magazines, leaflets and booklets for distribution to the population. Many of them are seized immediately by the racist regimes and banned from circulation, and very often the authors are arrested or harassed under the numerous security laws. Literature from liberation movements whenever circumstances allow usually sells like hot cakes because the question of liberation is a fundamental and ever-topical issue among all thinking Africans and other freedom-loving people. It is a popular cause.

When the liberation movement is proscribed so that nothing under its name can legally be published, trade unions, student unions and other patriotic organisations of the people remain the main channels through which information can be disseminated among the people. In most cases members, activists and officials of these organisations are also members of the liberation movement. The liberation movement is proscribed by the government when the struggle becomes intensified or reaches a more advanced stage. The more the racist governments feel threatened, the more repressive they become and the more repressive they become in desperation, the more they alienate the populace. At this stage the liberation movement increasingly becomes dependent on foreign radio stations, illegally and secretly produced leaflets and papers for general distribution. Or if produced outside the country, these papers can then be smuggled inside through many channels which the government cannot successfully check.

A pamphlet can be read by tens of people who informally spread the information to thousands of others. In spite of stiff laws which exist to deal with people who write or print or distribute "illegal" or "subversive" material, it has not proved possible to stop the flow completely. The determination of the people is too great to allow the enemy to fully succeed.

Foreign radio broadcasts are sometimes jammed by the racist regimes, but again this has not been successful because some foreign stations are too powerful to be effectively jammed. In Rhodesia, for instance, one can be arrested for listening to foreign broadcasts, especially those of the liberation movement, but still people continue to listen clandestinely in great numbers. These foreign broadcasts serve as tremendous sources of inspiration and hope for the oppressed. The broadcasters are usually members of the liberation movements in exile. For Zimbabwe, Azania and Namibia, Radios Tanzania, Zambia, Cairo, Ghana, Algeria, Congo and others have been used by the liberation movements. These broadcasting stations carry programmes run by the movements specially beamed to these minority-ruled countries. The programmes range from 30 to 90 minutes a day. They are aimed at informing the population about the progress of the struggle, how anybody can join and contribute, analysing current political developments, counteracting enemy propaganda, reiterating and clarifying the aims of the struggle and generally keeping the morale of the people high.

International propaganda is also a special concern of the liberation movements. Some is organised by the liberation movements themselves, some by solidarity and sympathetic groups, organisations and individuals at their own expense. Socialist countries and many progressive states have special radio programmes (some of which are beamed to Southern Africa), newspaper articles and pamphlets in support of the liberation struggles. This they do as their internationalist duty with their own money. Socialist countries which remain true to their original principles have a duty to support the world anti-imperialist revolution morally and materially. Without their support many African and other Third World countries would not have liberated themselves from colonialism and racial oppression at the time and in the way they did. Socialist countries, progressive states and the liberation movements of Africa are united by their hatred of imperialism in its different forms. The struggle against imperialist exploitation and for total liberation is the banner under which their politicised revolutionary peoples are united.

Serious liberation movements establish fraternal links with socialist and progressive governments, foreign sympathetic and solidarity groups and organisations and anti-colonialist journalists and politicians. The movements regularly furnish them with information and make sure that they are encouraged to publicise the progress of the struggle and thus isolate and demoralise the minority regimes and their sympathisers. At the same time, the solidarity groups, progressive organisations and all other freedom loving people internationally can also use the information from liberation movements for raising political consciousness among their own people for their own national struggle. The struggle against oppression in Southern Africa is in fact an integral part of the international fight against the exploitation of man by man. Its success in one part of the world is a victory for the exploited, wherever they are. A struggle against major British firms by British workers, for instance, is of great interest and a source of inspiration to the people of Southern Africa and many other parts of the world. The same British firms are so international in their operations that they are a common enemy of the people of

111

Southern Africa and elsewhere. Wherever they have their normal operations, they work under and in collaboration with the capitalist regime of the country. Those fighting against the capitalist government of that particular state find it necessary to coordinate their struggle with people engaged in, or who have gone through similar struggles.

On the part of the liberation movement, what is important is to have a clear understanding of the importance of the international mass media, good organisation and ability to set and constantly follow through correct priorities. Every liberation struggle, no matter what stage it is at, must have allies internationally. It is a matter of the liberation movement looking for them, establishing links, furnishing these sympathisers with information regularly and appealing to them to use the information in their mass media and other channels of communication. That cannot cost the liberation movement much. But one of the important prerequisites to the success of the liberation movement in this field is that those approached must respond promptly with the maximum material and financial support needed for the purpose. In fact, solidarity groups, movements, socialist and progressive governments and all freedom living people internationally should not wait to be approached for assistance. They can take the initiative and approach the liberation movements too. It is their revolutionary, internationalist and soildarity duty to do so, indeed, if they are really true to their principles.

It is imperative that journalists, writers, commentators and politicians interested in international affairs should always be fully supplied with information from the movement. The diplomatic struggle is an important aspect of the struggle as a whole. It should never be neglected. To the extent that a movement is internationally unknown or misunderstood, to that extent it is unlikely to receive international moral and material support to supplement the internal struggle. If a movement is not a secret society and yet it is internationally unknown or misunderstood or receives negative, or no publicity from the left and the freedom loving world, then there is something wrong with the way such a movement is run, or it has confused its priorities, or its supposed international allies are being outmanoeuvred by the right-wing and the retrogressive forces internationally. It must be emphasised, however, that information work is not the number-one priority of a liberation movement, nor can it be the main form of struggle against the enemy. It is clearly, though, one of the priorities and is an essential part of the process of liberation. In a coup d'etat, information work is important only during the take-over act, which can be accomplished overnight. The new government needs to be understood favourably by the population in order to consolidate the power of the new rulers. But a liberation movement needs a strong propaganda machinery before and after defeating the enemy. A revolutionary educational process is essential. The minds of the people have to be prepared so that they may fully participate and control their own struggle. They have to be made ready for a new and different society. Many of their old attitudes must be discarded and replaced with new ones which are more conducive to the blossoming of the new revolutionary era.

The media of communication throughout this whole transitionary period before and after liberation remain a powerful force as educator, mobiliser and organiser of the people. The media are a wide-scale and powerful socialising agency. That is why the minority regimes and their allies use them maximally. The more advanced and efficiently run the liberation movement is, the more that movement uses the information media, both clandestinely and publicly and also both internally and externally.

NOTES AND REFERENCES

1. Correspondent's report, 'South Africa Defends Policies at UN', *Financial Times*, London, 25 October 1974.
2. Reuter's report, 'Vorster Says Thank You Britain,' *The Guardian*, London, 6 November 1974.

3. *House of Assembly Debates* (Hansard), February 18, 1976, Questions and Replies, Cols 261-63, quoted in *Review of Recent Developments in South Africa* by Nicasio G. Valderrama, Centre Against Apartheid, UN, New York, 1976, page 6.
4. See Maxey, Kees: *From Rhodesia to Zimbabwe*, Fabian Society, London, 1972, Chapter 6.
5. See Andrew Wilson's article, 'Why the US Tilted Towards Vorster', *The Observer*, London, 5 January 1975 (an analysis of the US policy document entitled National Security Study Memorandum 39, of 1969).
6. Mario Soares, *The Decolonization of Territories Under Portuguese Administration*, an address to the UN General Assembly on 23 September 1974, published in *Objective: Justice*, New York, vol.6, no.4, October/November/ December 1974, p.3.
7. See Benjamin Pogrund's article, 'Pastor Tells Why Blacks Are Fleeing', *Daily Telegraph*, London, 3 November 1974.
8. See survey of *The Sunday Times* Insight team, 'Rhodesia: Why the "Friendly" South Africans Want to Retire to the Laager', *The Sunday Times*, 15 December 1974.
9. Document 53B, Annual Reports of the Secretary of Defence, 1967-1971 (CSR 25-1968, 21-1969, CMDRR 15-1971, 16-1972), pp282-5, and see also Peter Nieswand's article, 'Rhodesia: What Smith Really Faces', in *The Rhodesian Problem*, op cit, pp296-303.
10. An article by David Holden, 'South Africa Ready to Tell Smith: You're on Your Own', *The Sunday Times*, London, October 13, 1974.
11. See Survey of *The Sunday Times* Insight team, op.cit.
12. Summary of report made on 14 February 1975 to the 24th session of the Council of Ministers of OAU by John Malecela, Minister of Foreign Affairs, Tanzania, in Tanzania.
13. *Lusaka Manifesto*, OAU, Addis Ababa, September 1969, p4.
14. A correspondent's report, 'Moderate Africans Backed on Policy Towards Mr Vorster', *The Times*, London, 10 April 1975. Also see AP report, 'South Africa Promises to Withdraw Its Forces by End of May, *The Times*, London 9 April 1975.
15. Neal Ascherson, 'The Flaws in Vorster's Grand Design', *The Observer*, London, 13 April 1975.
16. News agencies report, 'Vorster Pledge on Peace', *The Guardian*, London, 21 February 1975.
17. *The Star*, Johannesburg, weekly airmail edition, May 8, 1976, quoted in *Review of Recent Developments in South Africa*, 1976, ibid.
18. Ginwala, Frene: *The Press in South Africa*, Unit on Apartheid, United Nations, New York, 1972, pages 19-20.
19. Tabel-Bendiab, Mokhtar: *South African Propaganda*, Centre Against Apartheid, United Nations, New York, 1976, page 4.
20. Kahana, Shafashike: *Mass Media in Namibia*, an article in *The Democratic Journalist*, Prague, No. 5, 1976, pages 14-17.
21. See Windrich, Ellaine: *The Rhodesian Problem*, Routledge and Kegan Paul, London, 1975, part 5.
22. See Maxey, Kees: op cit, page 12.

Chapter 5:
Suppression of Dissent and the Durability of White Rule

In order to maintain white supremacy through the apartheid
and Bantustan policy, repressive legislation and measures had
to be instituted in the name of "law and order and white
Christian civilisation and the security of the state."(1) Among
the many laws which give wide powers to the police are the
Criminal Procedure and Evidence Act (No 29 of 1955) and
the Criminal Procedure Act (No 56 of 1955), under which
the police are allowed to make searches without warrant,
attend any private and public meetings, and enter any premises to find documents. Every day 2,500 Africans are
arrested and sentenced for breaking the pass laws alone,
which determine where one can work and reside. The average
time taken to handle these cases is 2 minutes. To be aquitted
in court does not necessarily mean freedom; that will depend
on whether the court's judgement coincides with the wishes
of the security police and the Minister of Justice. (1)

The apartheid system is more and more stifling opposition
from both whites and blacks. All opposition — liberal, black
nationalist, communist or religious — is suppressed. A poster
published by a group of church men in South Africa draws
attention to how all kinds of dissent are being muzzled:(2)

"In 1950, they came for the Communists:
I was not a Communist and it did not concern me.
In 1953, they came for the Trade Unionists:
I was not a Trade Unionist and it did not concern me.

In 1955, they took the vote from the Coloured people:
I was not Coloured and it did not concern me.

They came for the African Nationalists:
I was not an African Nationalist and it did not concern me.
They imposed censorship legislation:
I was not a writer and it did not concern me.

In 1968, they passed the Improper Interference Bill:
I was not in the Liberal Party and it did not concern me.
In 1972, they began trial by commision:
I was not affected and it did not concern me.
In 1973, they banned white and black student leaders:
I was not a student and it did not concern me.

Now they are coming for Christian and social change groups:
I am a member of these, but there is nobody left to support me.
When will they come for you?"

The South African security forces can make anyone disappear any time. The number of such missing persons even according to official figures is staggering — and to these must be added an uncountable host who simply are ghosted away without their relatives, friends or the press being informed of their whereabouts or the charges against them. To elicit information about people who disappear or who are known to be detainees or prisoners is one of the most difficult tasks of the press. Not only can the police refuse to cooperate, but the reporter and his newspaper may also find themselves in trouble for being "too nosey". It is generally expedient not to bother about or report such issues, in case one ends up in court.

After arrest, maximum torture is customarily applied to get information or make the detainee sign a false and self-incriminating statement. The Christian Institute of South Africa compiled a report, which was immediately banned by the government, based on affidavits of people appearing in court.(3)   The affidavits show beyond any reasonable doubt that the security forces use the following methods of torturing their victims:

- holding the head under water in a lavatory;
- applying electric shocks to the genitals and other parts of the body;
- deprivation of sleep;
- making the victim stand blindfolded for many days and nights;
- assaulting prisoners.

Many people die in prison as a result of this kind of treatment.

Between June and October 1976 alone, 226 bodies in government mortuaries had gunshot wounds. Professor Joshua Taljaard, South Africa's state pathologist, told Mr Justice Cillie, head of a government commission, that more than half of the black people shot by the South African police were shot in the back. (3)

The tables below show that South Africa has one of the highest (in proportion to population) figures for imprisonment in the world.(4) Here it is compared with England and Wales.

The Total Population of Each Racial Group in South Africa Compared With the Population of Such Groups in Prison in 1969

	Africans	Whites	Coloured	Asians
% of the total population of South Africa	68	19	10	3
% of admissions under sentence for year ended 30.6.1969	85.5	1.5	12.5	0.3
% of persons in prison as at 30.6.1969	78.5	3	18.5	0.3

Admissions to Prison for Selected Years 1912 to 1969

Year	Population of South Africa	Total Admissions (including remands)	Column 3 as % of Column 2	Admissions on Sentence
1912	6,100,000	120,894	2%	95,822
1922	7,100,000	127,875	1.8%	96,722
1932	8,300,000	202,276	2.4%	172,555
1942	10,800,000	199,708	1.9%	151,922
1952	13,500,000	265,000	2%	201,000
1962	17,200,000	461,000	2.7%	347,000
1965	18,500,000	411,000	2.3%	285,000
1968	19,800,000	665,000	3.4%	486,000
1969	20,300,000	658,000	3.2%	496,000

NUMBER OF PRISONERS: 1964

	No. of Prisoners	Total Population
South Africa	297,000	18,000,000
England and Wales	53,000	46,000,000

Giving evidence to the Cillie Commission set up to investigate the causes of riots in Soweto and other areas of the country in October 1976, Mr I.W. Ackerman, Chief Director of the Highveld Bantu Administration Board, stated that "freedom of the press" had played a major role in sparking off the troubles. Church leaders opposed to apartheid, he explained, should also be made to keep quiet.[5] From the establishment point of view the situation demands increased repression and not relaxation. Once the ruling class starts systematically repressing its own members it is in for trouble.

The stronger the liberation struggle becomes, the more contradictions develop within the ruling class. As always, the more threatened a ruling class is, the more brutal it becomes and suppresses an increasingly big number of its own members. The more repressive it becomes, the more determined the oppressed people become. The more determined they are, getting better organised as an opposition movement, the more they increase the insecurity of the ruling class. The more brutal and fascistic the enemy becomes, the more internationally isolated does it find itself. The more isolated the enemy becomes, the more demoralised, insecure, divided and confused it grows. The more that happens, the shorter its life-expectation becomes, and consequently the nearer comes victory for the oppressed.

In a social system where there is a "consensus," repression tends to be kept to a minimum. Whereas, in a system where the opposition is growing threateningly and openly stronger, as is the case in South Africa, the system tends to become more repressive. But when repression of members of the opposition begins to include people who are normally supporters, or members of the ruling class, then that system can not survive for long. This is what is now happening in South Africa. A systematic and continuous increase in the massive suppression of internal dissent is a sign of weakness on the part of the ruling class. It mirrors a vote of no confidence by the majority of the citizens of the country against their rulers.

White power as minority, racist and decadent capitalist power has a rotten core. It is being attacked from within and from without, nationally and internationally. The liberationist groups and organisations are recognised by United Nations organisations, the Organization of African Unity and other international bodies. The South African racist regime has become an international outcast. More than 95% of the UN members, including the big powers, have denounced the politics of the South African government of Vorster. The three statements reproduced below, which are in accord with the spirit and content of this study, show the reasons for the international ostracisation of South Africa. The majority of the UN members would take the same view.

"The surge towards national sovereignty and independence in Africa, which has been one of the most important historical developments in this century, cannot and will not be checked.

Therefore, the question is not whether those peoples still under colonial control will become independent but when and under what circumstances. . .

"The international community cannot be indifferent to the situation in those areas. In particular, the United Nations, which has played so central a role in the process of decolonisation, having endorsed the cause of the liberation movement, must not be indifferent. . . "

Kurt Waldheim, UN Secretary General (6)

"Suffice it to say that apartheid is the subjection of the great majority of the people of South Africa to discrimination, segregation, exploitation and humiliation. It is not only an intolerable affront to human dignity, but a crime against humanity. . .

"It is today the concern of humanity, an urgent and inescapable concern of the United Nations. It is, and must be, as much a concern of Europe, North America as of Asia and Africa. . .

"Of far more significance than the geographical location of South Africa is the fact that it is the purposes and principles of the United Nations which are at stake."

Ambassador Edwin Ogebe Ogbu (Nigeria),
Chairman of the UN Special Committee on Apartheid (7)

"As to what is wrong with apartheid — the concept of human rights derives from the universal acceptance of a fundamental moral principle — the dignity and worth of the human person, which lies, incidentally, at the very heart of the Christian religion professed by the Irish people. Apartheid is in its essence an attack on the very basis of human rights, in that it attempts to establish two kinds of human rights, those for whites and those for non-whites, in short, two categories of humanity. Such an attack on the very basis of human morality is repugnant to the citizens of a world which has increasingly come to realize its inter-dependence and to accept the universal and categorical moral obligations which are enshrined in the Charter of the United Nations."

Dr Garret FitzGerald,

Minister for Foreign Affairs of Ireland (8)

The OAU and the UNO have taken a strong stand against the Bantustan policies of South Africa. This has done a lot to expose and frustrate South Africa's diplomatic and international propaganda offensive.

The Council of Ministers of the OAU in its ninth extraordinary session, in Dar-es-Salaam from 7 to 10 April 1975 decided "to reiterate its condemnation and rejection of any Bantustan policy and practice and call on all United Nations Member-States to desist from establishing any contacts with the Homeland 'leaders' .... " (UN Notes and Documents, No. 19/75).

When the Bantustan of Transkei was granted "independence" by South Africa on October 16, 1976 the UN General Assembly voted 134 against recognition with one abstention. The General Assembly resolution 31/6A, inter alia:

"1. Strongly condemns the establishment of bantustans as designed to consolidate the inhuman policies of apartheid, to destroy the territorial integrity of the country, to perpetuate white minority domination and to dispossess the African people of South Africa of their inalienable rights;

"2. Rejects the declaration of 'independence' of the Transkei and declares it invalid;

"3. Calls upon all Governments to deny any form of recognition to the so-called independent Transkei and to refrain from having any dealing with the so-called independent Transkei or other bantustans."

Up to July 1977, no other country had extended diplomatic recognition to Transkei except the government of South Africa.

The following are some of the most well-known international organisations from which South Africa was forced to withdraw or was expelled from membership:

1. International Labour Organisation (ILO).
2. Food and Agricultural Organization of the UN.

3. United Nations Educational, Scientific and Cultural Organisation.

By 1976 South Africa's membership was threatened in many international organisations to which it belonged, including the United Nations Organisation. Its credentials as an internationally accepted independent and civilised nation were seriously questioned in view of its intolerably abhorrent racist policies. The credit for this international ostracisation should go first to the people inside South Africa who are fighting for their liberation. Their efforts to free themselves under such circumstances have been found to be impossible to check by the South African government; nor can information about the progress of their struggle and the damage being inflicted on the apartheid edifice be suppressed any longer. The reason is simply that the struggle inside South Africa has reached another, new, crucial and higher stage. This stage is so advanced that the international community not only must notice it, but has to decide on which side it is to align itself. Secondly, credit must go to the banned liberation movements still operating from abroad, which enlisted the support of the socialist countries and other progressive forces and nations, in order to launch an anti-racist and international diplomatic offensive. This offensive has helped to expose the South African system, pass international resolutions against it, and organise diplomatic, trade, cultural and other boycotts. Apart from trying to organise and prepare for guerrilla warfare inside South Africa, the anit-South African diplomatic work is one of the major tasks that the South African exiled liberation organisations have undertaken.

Turning South Africa into an international outcast has a direct bearing on the struggle inside South Africa. When the liberationists inside the country hear what the attitude of the outside world would be to their struggle and what is being done internationally against the South African government, they feel encouraged, their morale soars, and it becomes easy for them to get much needed external moral, diplomatic and material assistance. This information, as has been stated earlier, reaches them through newspapers, radio broadcasts, leaflets and other papers smuggled into the country. The media, both external and internal, continuously play an important role in the development of the consciousness of the people and the struggle in general.

It is also recognised by most of the liberationists that the main struggle is inside South Africa, not outside. Mobilising international support, which must be done in most cases by solidarity groups and not as a preoccupation of any genuine national liberation movement, is an important, but supplementary part of the total struggle. The main effort of a liberation movement should be directed at the main form of struggle — the armed struggle at the present stage of the history of South Africa.

In this second half of the twentieth century, the myth of the durability of white minority racist power in South Africa is being thoroughly exposed, both inside the country and overseas. No matter what military might the regime may possess and how brutally it may use its security forces to muzzle the aspirations of the majority, the South African system has clearly become an anachronism internationally which cannot go on for ever.

NOTES AND REFERENCES

1. See Carlson, Joel: *South Africa — A Police State,* Unit on Apartheid, UN, New York, October 1973; also a study by the International Commission of Jurists, "Infringements of the Universal Declaration of Human Rights in South Africa", *Objective: Justice,* Vol. 5, no. 4, October 1973, Unit on Apartheid, UN, New York.
2. Quoted by the Rev. Canon L. John Collins in his statement before the special session of the UN Special Committee on Apartheid in Dublin, 20 May 1974, published June 1974 as *Document no 12/74,* UN Unit on Apartheid, New York.
3. See *Information Bulletin on Political Prisoners and Detainees,* ANC of South Africa, London, October 1976.
4. Friedman, Julian, *Basic Facts on the Republic of South Africa and the Policy of Apartheid,* Unit on Apartheid, New York, August 1974, pages 35 and 38.
5. See article by Nicholas Ashford: *The Times,* London, October 27, 1976.
6. Kurt Waldheim, in a statement to the UN Special Committee on Decolonization on 29 January, 1974, published in *Decolonization,* UN Department of Political Affairs, Trusteeship and Decoloniization, New York, Vol. 1, no. 1, June 1974, page 1.
7. H.E. Mr. Edwin Ogebe Ogbu, *No Compromise with Apartheid,* address to the solemn meeting of the UN Special Committee on the International Day for the Elimination of Racial Discrimination, 21 March 1974, published by UN Unit for Apartheid, Department of Political and Security Council Affairs, April 1974, New York, page 1.
8. FitzGerald, Garret: *Apartheid An Affront to Humanity,* Unit on Apartheid, UN, New York, July 1974, page 1.

Chapter 6:
Theories of Mass Communication

Having examined the political system, the state legislation and its implementation as major determinants of the role of the mass media as instruments of political change, it is appropriate now to assess the power of the mass media to influence or change attitudes and ideas of individuals — another major factor when looking at the limitations and possibilities of the mass media as instruments of political change in society.

Since mass communication media were developed as important social institutions, they have been fairly consistently blamed for increasing crime, violence, immorality, escapism, political demoralisation and subversion. Charges and counter-charges, usually based on inconclusive evidence, are frequently bandied about. Those accusers of and apologists for the mass media more often than not ignore the available evidence, which is the result of decades of scientific research into the effects and role of the mass media in society. (1) Summaries of the research and surveys on the effects of mass communication media are well documented. (2)

As a complex organised entity, society in the way we know it today cannot exist without communication, so communication processes must therefore have an effect on the socio-political system. Modern political activity would be impossible without the modern forms of mass communcation geared to such society. This is the basis of the time-honoured argument between politicians and journalists. When Vice

President of the US Spiro Agnew,(3) on 13th November 1969, was blaming American television for the "credibility gap" between the people and the government, he stated that ". . . this little group of men who not only enjoy right of instant rebuttal to every Presidential address, but more importantly wield a free hand in selecting, presenting and interpreting the great issues in our nation. . . They decide what 40 to 50 million Americans will learn of the day's events in the nation and the world. We cannot measure this power and influence by the traditional democratic standards, for these men create national issues overnight. They can make or break by their coverage and commentary, a moratorium on the war. They can elevate men from obscurity to national importance within a week. They can reward some politicians with national exposure and ignore others. . . Is it not fair and relevant to question its concentration in the hands of a tiny enclosed fraternity of privileged men elected by no one and enjoying a monopoly sanctioned and licensed by government?" Within a month, the speech provoked 80,000 letters to Agnew supporting his stand; the media received 150,000 letters, in a proportion of two-to-one in favour of Agnew.

The role of the media has always been a controversial topic because the power or effect of the media cannot be considered in isolation from other factors in society and cannot be conclusively measured. The effects are diverse and complex. They vary according to the nature of relationships within society – relationships between individuals, institutions or groups and the political system – and there are many possible combinations, depending upon an endless range of questions.(4) The effects can be direct or secondary; immediate or supplementary; general or specific; lasting or restricted in time; profound or fleeting; comprehensive or isolated; original or mediated; stimulating or inconsequential. There are numerous further variants. "All political effects are initially upon individuals", says Seymour-Ure, "They consist in increments of information which may or may not modify attitudes which may or may not modify behaviour."(5)

Summarising Joseph T. Klapper's work on the effects of mass communication, J.D. Halloran (6) has come up with these tentative generalisations:

"1.   Mass communication ordinarily does not serve as a necessary and sufficient cause of audience effect, but rather functions among and through a nexus of mediating factors and influences.

2.   These mediating factors are such that they typically render mass communication a contributing agent, but not the sole cause in a process of reinforcing the existing conditions. (Regardless of the condition in question — be it the vote intentions of audience members, their tendency towards or away from delinquent behaviour, or their general orientation, towards life and its problems — and regardless of whether the effect in question be social of individual, the media are more likely to reinforce than to change.)

3.   On such occasions as mass communication does function in the service of change, one of the two conditions is likely to exist. Either:

(a)   the mediating factors will be found to be inoperative and the effect of the media will be found to be direct; or

(b)   the mediating factors, which normally favour reinforcements, will be found to be themselves impelling towards change.

4.   There are certain residual situations in which mass communication seems to produce direct effects, or directly and of itself to serve certain psycho-physical functions.

5.   The efficacy of mass communciation, either as a contributory agent or as an agent of direct effect, is affected by various aspects of the media and communications themselves or of the communication situations (including, for example, aspects of textual organisation, the nature of the source and medium, the existing climate of public opinion, and the like)."

Klapper himself accepts that these generalisations are not all-covering, suggest further research possibilities and have the inherent danger of making one become preoccupied with a study of the mediating factors and thus divert from the original goal or ignore the fact that mass communication media have their own unique qualities and could have characteristic effects. These generalisations, however, are useful in bringing order into a field which has not yet been as thoroughly researched as other disciplines.(6)

Behavioural, especially political change is a slow and difficult process. A human being normally strives for consistency, balance and congruity. Nan Lin(7) has put forward three main reasons why change is slow and difficult: "man's basic need for psychological or cognitive closure; the tight ring of his social reinforcement; and his self-fulfilling communication behaviour." Change is the contradiction or modification of a person's past behaviour. People have a tendency to avoid unsympathetic material — unsympathetic to their existing opinions. They forget unsympathetic material more easily than the material which is in accord with their current beliefs. Two decades of research have shown that mass communication media have a tendency to reinforce existing attitudes and ideas rather than directly to change them. (8) Change is more likely to occur through interpersonal communication than through mass communication alone. The mass media are not as directly effective as they might be because people have selective exposure, selective retention, and selective perception (interpretation). Unlike inter-personal communication, mass communication is not immediate (but impersonal) and does not facilitate immediate feedback and immediate response. In inter-personal communication there is encounter and exchange of ideas and attitudes which is direct and more effective communication than mass communication. Melvin C. DeFleur(9) has summed up contemporary thinking about the effects of the mass media of communication into four specific formulations, set out below.

The individual differences theory
The individual differences theory is based on the fact that human beings are different from each other. They have different experiences, attitudes and habits, and are different

in psychological structure. Not all individuals can be motivated or influenced at the same time by the same persuasive communication. The audience is not uniform. The effects of mass communication therefore vary from person to person according to the individual's personality structure.

The social categories theory

This theory assumes that people can be put into broad collectives, aggregates or social categories whose reaction to given stimuli is more or less uniform. Age, sex, income level, educational attainment, residence and religious affiliation are some of the relevant examples. A certain group or social category is likely to select more or less the same communication content and may react to it in more or less the same way. Psychologists have tended to favour the individual differences theory and sociologists the social categories theory. Together, the two theories influence researchers to take into account the social differentiation of society and the individual differences of personality. The two theories were embodied in 1948 in Lasswell's paradigm of the communication process:

who
says what
in what channel
to whom
with what effect.

The social relationships theory

Informal social relationships play an important part in modifying the manner or behaviour of an individual and how he/she will act upon certain mass communication content. Information comes from the media to relatively well-informed persons who will in turn through inter-personal channels pass on the information coupled with their own interpretations to members of their social group who have less direct exposure to the media. The people in contact with the media in these social groups are called "opinion leaders"; this kind of communication process is called the "two-step flow" of communication.

The cultural norms theory

This theory postulates that the media through selective presentations and emphasis of certain themes create impressions among the people that common cultural norms are structured or defined in some specific way. Mass communication can help reinforce existing patterns and lead people to believe that particular social norms are maintained by society. The mass media can help to create new shared convictions on topics of which the public has little or no prior knowledge. The media can contribute to the change of existing norms, which can lead people from one form of behaviour to another. In a situation like the South African one, the "opinion leaders" in the white community are mostly those who support the status quo. They receive information direct from the various information media, digest it, re-interpret it and then pass it on to their social group and community when it is already blended with their own conclusions and exhortations in support of the system. At this stage the information is generally disseminated through direct person-to-person channels of communication. In the black community, the process is similar. The "opinion leaders" are people who mostly support the liberation struggle. They are the activists and liberationists. They are a product of the material conditions of their community. They are thrown up by the struggle to safeguard and promote the interests and aspirations of their community. They also pass on much of the information through word of mouth.

Conclusion

The major difficulty in any attempt to unravel the role of the mass media in political change is that there are so many factors involved. As a contributory agent, the effectiveness of the mass media cannot be conclusively determined, nor should it be over-emphasised. Even if it were legally possible to use the mass media in South Africa as an instrument of political change, as we have seen the extent of their influence would be limited by the fact that people do not change their ideas simply because the media content is persuasive, convincing and in favour of change. Thus, although the majority of the white newspaper readers in South Africa take the English newspapers, they still vote for the National Party. As has been shown, people choose what they want to read, interpret the contents differently and usually in favour of the status quo if they believe that the status quo protects their interests better as individuals or as a group — in the case of South Africa as a ruling racial group. Since the people who believe in their racial superiority own and control the mass media in South Africa, they have enacted laws aimed at consolidating minority rule and the present economic system; the mass media can not, therefore, under the circumstances, be used openly as an effective instrument of political change, despite the belief of many of the white journalists and politicians in South Africa and others abroad that there is freedom of the press in South Africa. By virtue of its history, pattern of ownership, the laws under which it operates and the political and commercial forces it represents, the English-language papers can be used only for campaigning for minor political changes and liberalisation which would not on their own culminate in that type of political transformation that would restore political rights and allow adult suffrage to all the inhabitants of South Africa. While one can conclude from the evidence given in this book that under the present circumstances one should not expect much from the South African mass media, even the English-language papers, as far as their contribution to the process of political change is concerned, it is important, however, to note that the process of political change is so complex, with so many militating factors involved, that the movements for change should not exclude the possibility of ever using the mass media, particularly the English-language papers, on a significant scale. Circumstances cannot remain static permanently; contradictions among the forces of reaction and retrogression provide possibilities for getting the message through to more sections of the population, winning new allies and eventually weakening and destroying the old socio-economic system so that a new, humane and democratic one can be established. However, as at present, the important aspect of the English-language papers is likely to continue to be that of a leading barometer for measuring the level of contradictions and other developments within the white ruling class, which can be of relevance or use to the many groups and movements struggling at various levels for human dignity, freedom and the democratisation of society.

While trying their best to use the enemy media of information and those of their allies wherever feasible, the liberationists concentrate on using and developing their own to the maximum level possible. This approach is part of the philosophy of self-reliance followed by every serious and genuine liberationist group. Using only the enemy media, whenever the opportunity arises, and those of the supporters of liberation struggle externally is not only insufficient, but can have the effect of robbing the movement of its right to be original and self-reliant, and of the chance to develop its own talent and structures and of using primarily its own resources. A balance has to be struck and priority given to the movement's own information media on most occasions.

NOTES AND REFERENCES

1. See Halloran, J.D.: *The Effects of Mass Communication, With Special Reference to Television*, Leicester University Press, 1971, page 11.
2. The following list, which is not necessarily a complete one, contains summaries of the research and surveys undertaken on the effects of mass communication: Halloran in *The Effects of Mass Communication, With Special Reference to Television*, ibid; J.D. Halloran in *The Effects of Television*, 1970; Colin Seymour-Ure in *The Political Impact of Mass Media, 1974*; J.T. Klapper in *The Effects of Mass Communication*, 1960; M.L. DeFleur in *Theories of Mass Communication*, 1966; J. Tunstall (ed) in *Media Sociology*, 1970; D. Chaney in *Processes of Mass Communication*, 1972; Walter Weiss in *The Effects of the Mass Media of Communication* in G. Lindzey and E. Aronson's *Handbook of Social Psychology*, vol. 5, 1969 (5 vols); W. Schramm in *Mass Media in National Development*, 1964; and Denis McQuail in *Towards a Sociology of Mass Communications*, 1969.
3. Smith, Antony: *The Shadow in the Cave: The Broadcaster, the Audience, and the State*, George Allen & Unwin, London, 1973, preface.
4. See Seymour-Ure, Colin: *The Political Impact of Mass Media*, Constable, London, 1974, especially pages 44, 62, 63.
5. Seymour-Ure, Colin: ibid, page 62.
6. Halloran, J.D.: op.cit, pages 30, 31.
7. Lin, Nan, *The Study of Human Communication*, Babbs-Merrill, New York, 1973, page 176.
8. See Klapper, Joseph T.: *The Effects of Mass Communication*, The Free Press, New York, 1960, chapter 2, and also Nan Lin, ibid, chapter 6.
9. DeFleur, Melvin L.: op cit, chapter 8.

Appendix 1
SASO Statement

(An address to the Cape Town University students
by B.A. Khoapa of the South African Students'
Organization, reproduced from the *Azania News*,
January–March 1975)

When your SRC president invited me to come here and talk to
you, I replied that I did not feel it a great priority of mine to
do so, for I belong to a group of people who are seeing increasingly the futility of devoting a major portion of their
time to talking and intellectualising about things that prove
unhelpful to both sides because we see things differently.
Your president did not agree with me and he argued that
there is some value in getting white students at least to be
aware of the things that make people (black and white) in
this country see things differently and he assured me that
white students at this university would benefit something
from what I have to say. I finally agreed to come here today
and talk to you with the full understanding that I do not
believe that what I say here is necessarily going to be useful
for the group I am most concerned about, that is, black
people. But if you benefit anything from what I am about
to say to you, well and good; if you don't, I will not hold it
against you because it will prove what I said earlier, that it is
not possible for you and me to see things the same way until
we have redefined a few things. Feel free therefore to walk
out just as soon as you think you cannot take it any longer.

I feel that it is important however to state very clearly
where some of us stand at this time in our history. Very
often the viewpoint of the so-called 'militant black' has been
so badly misunderstood that it becomes necessary to explain
it for the benefit of those who are interested in understanding
it sincerely. I will attempt to do this now and in doing so I
will start first of all by looking at two concepts which have

bedevilled this country for many years. The concepts I refer to are integration and separation.

Very often it is assumed that if a person is not an 'integrationist' in South Africa he is therefore a 'separatist' and that because an increasing number of black people are rejecting 'integration' as a national goal, they are therefore 'separatist', that is, they make the permanent separation of races a national goal. This is nonsense. The black people who have been accused of being 'separatist' are in fact not 'separatists' but liberationists. Central to both separation and integration is the white man. Blacks must either move towards or away from him. But his presence is not nearly so crucial for those who pursue a course of 'liberation'. Ideally they do whatever they conceive they must do as if whites did not exist at all. At the very least the minds of the 'new black' are liberated from the patterns programmed there by a society built on the alleged aesthetic, moral and intellectual superiority of the white man.

Liberationists contend that integration is irrelevant to a people who are powerless. For them the equitable distribution of decision-making power is far more important than physical proximity to white people. This means complete emancipation of blacks from white oppression by whatever means blacks deem necessary, including, when expedient, integration or separation. What the new black man is talking about is liberation by any means necessary and this does not depend on whether blacks should integrate or separate. The fundamental issue is not separation or integration. The either/or question does not therefore talk to the point that the new black is making. We will use the word regroupment to refer to that necessary process of development every oppressed group must travel en route to emancipation.

What people always call separation in the black community is not separation but regroupment. It is not separation for blacks to come together on matters of common policy. It is not separation for blacks to go together on Sunday to a church which has never been closed to anyone. It is not separation for blacks to go into a room, shut the door, and hammer out a common policy. I would like to explain why a liberationist gets irritated by the constant accusation that he should either be for separation or for integration or otherwise be a fraud. This kind of either/or thing is irrelevant and a waste of time and energy and I will say why.

First, the either/or thing is irrelevant or immaterial: because it confuses means and ends, strategy and tactics; it makes a fetish out of mere words and offers a pre-determined response for every place and time. What is to be done? — that depends — depends on what? — on what advances the cause of black liberation. The question of the presence or absence of white people is a tactical matter which can only be answered in a concrete situation by reference to the short-term or long-term interests of the blacks. The tactics will depend on the situation and will flow naturally from that situation if people will only remember that the aim is not to separate or integrate but to triumph.

The second reason why I say that this either/or proposition is irrelevant is because it is based on false premises. It assumes that blacks are free to choose and that their only options are the horns of a dilemma. This assumption does not do full justice to the complexity and the tragedy of the black man's situation. It ignores the infinite gradations between integration and separation and the fact that there is a third choice — pluralism, and beyond that the fourth — transformation. Even more serious is the hidden assumption that blacks are free to choose ex nihilo. But the essence of our situation at this moment is that we can neither separate nor integrate. We are caught just now in an impossible historical situation and that fact, which terrifies some, and leads others to despair, gives our struggle a grandeur, a nobility, and a certain tragedy which makes it of moment to the world.

It is impossible to draw a straight line on a curved space. Both 'integrationists' and 'separatists' are trying to create right angles in a situation which only permits curves. The only option is transformation of a situation which does not permit a clear-cut choice in either direction. The philosophy of liberation recognises this fact and suggests that we use history as an instrument of appraisal and analysis. It points out that all movements of liberation in the black community, whether of integration or of separation, have failed, and asks why? What were the movement's strong points and weak points? What mistakes were made and what can we learn from those mistakes? Another evasion of the mistake situation is to assume that the blacks can integrate unilaterally, and from this assumption it is but one step from the pernicious idea that blacks are polarising the country. This is the same policy of giving a white disease a black name (the native problem) and blaming the oppressed for the oppressor's aggression. It is not separatism of blacks but the separatism of whites which threatens this country. The decision is in the hands of whites. If they want transformation, let them give up their separate neighbourhoods and institutions and organisations and come out into the open. Until then, blacks must organise and use their group strength to wrest control of every organisation and institution within reach.

The either/or thing proposition is false also because it is based on a misunderstanding of the modern world which is grounded on group power, group organisation and group conflict. This is a world of groups. A man's power depends ultimately on the power of his group. This means that oppressed individuals must recognise their common interests and create a group. Groupness is a simple exigency of the situation. The oppressor creates a situation from which the oppressed can only extricate themselves by a regroupment. From this sketch it is clear that the oppressor and the oppressed must clash. Some men try to avoid the exigencies of the situation by preaching universal brotherhood. But it is a mystification to preach universal brotherhood in a situation of oppression. Paradoxically, a prerequisite for human solidarity is a feeling of non-solidarity with men who stand in the way of solidarity. Paradoxically, the oppressed can only bring about a future of universal brotherhood in proportion as they feel and exhibit group solidarity among themselves and cease to feel solidarity with the enemies of human solidarity.

Indeed we shall earn the right to love all men by struggling against some; we shall earn the right to hold hands with all men by refusing to hold hands with all men who stand in the way of all men holding hands with all men. Here, as elsewhere, the devil must be driven out first; it is too soon to love everybody. This brings us to the paradox of integration; to the fact that the blacks must sing black and black together, before they can sing black and white together, to the fact that the black integration must precede black and white integration, to the fact that blacks must unite before they can separate and must separate before they can unite. There is nothing ominous or subversive about this principle. It is simply an exigency of the situation. History has charged us with the responsibility for going to the very gate of racism in order to destroy racism — to the gate not further.

The either/or proposition does not explicate the dialectics of development in which a negation is necessary for a synthesis. Sweet are the uses of 'integration'. The stress on black nationalism and black separation in white media is ideological; its function is to keep blacks unorganised and powerless. Whites have organised racially-oriented businesses, unions, churches, newspapers, resorts, country clubs, youth camps, welfare agencies, ethnic studies departments, colleges, universities, unmarried mothers' agencies, child welfare agencies, vacation associations, war veteran groups, professional association, employment services, theatres, encyclopaedias, funeral homes, homes for the aged, agricultural societies, boards, tourist agencies. But whites are always telling blacks that organisation on a national basis is a no-no. It is especially naughty for blacks to form organisations without white members and white officers.

Finally the either/or dilemma is irrelevant and immaterial because it is a reaction to an action. Both integration and separation are responses, and largely emotional responses at that, to white oppression. Neither integration nor separation deals with the question for both remain on the level defined by whites. Both integrationists and separatists are excessively pre-occupied with the question of sitting down beside the white man. The separatist is excessively pre-occupied with the question of not sitting down beside the white man. The liberationist says that the presence or absence of the white man is irrelevant. What obsesses him is the liberation of Black people, and the white man is free to aid that liberation by contributing information, sweat, money and blood, but he is not free to join that struggle or to lead it. Pre-occupation with the white man leads to blunders, confusion in the ranks, and demoralisation; it obscures the issues. It is possible, for example, to be free, creative and happy without being in the presence of white people. It is also possible to be free, creative and happy in groups which are not all black. Neither separation nor integration confronts the system in its totality for both share the same root postulates. In one or another both deplore the fact that white people do not love black people. But love is irrelevant. History is a struggle, not an orgy. Men decide matters of fundamental interest, not on the basis of goodwill, but on the basis of social necessity — on the basis of what they consider to be in their interests. Men do not and cannot love each other if their material interests conflict. As long as institutions, particularly economic instiutions, make it necessary for one group to hate another in order to maximise its position, then integration is impossible.

It is not necessary to argue the either/or question of whether racism is either economic or ideological. What is certain is that racial problems can only be solved in a climate of economic equality. The either integration or separation dilemma ignores the implications of this fact. One side ignores it by calling for 'integration' of the black man into the economic status quo. But the prerequisite for integration, that is, transformation, is the integration of the economic order. Most proponents of the either/or dilemma find such discussions tedious. Basically they are idealists; they believe that the words in the books mean something.

The philosophy of liberation calls for a transcendence of the either/or dilemma which has had such disastrous impact on white/black policy. The liberationist concedes the power of the integrationists' dream but points out that black power is necessary to accomplish it. A philosophy of liberation requires a frank appraisal of the institutions and policies of white communities. A philosophy of liberation also requires an advanced programme of economic democracy. Racial integration requires economic integration, and this in turn requires the recognition that the race problem cannot be solved without profound structural modifications in the country; without real changes in the tax structure and the relations between the private and public sectors; without a redifinition and a redistribution of income and power.

A philosophy of liberation requires a re-appraisal of the policies and institutions of the black community. We must re-evaluate everything we are doing and saying. We must rise now to the level of conceiving the black interest as the universal interest. Too many people think blackness means withdrawing and tightening the circle. On the contrary blackness means expanding and widening the circle; absorbing and integrating instead of being absorbed and integrated, and from that perspective, it is easy to see that a philosophy of liberation requires black people to cast their light, not over one thing, but over everything. We must rise now to the level of black hegemony; the idea that blacks must establish moral and cultural authority over the whole. A philosophy of liberation requires transformation. It says everything must be made anew but we recognise that blackness, as so many people have said, is necessary but not sufficient. Being black is not enough. One must be black and ready together.

A philosophy of liberation requires unity. Black unity in turn requires black organisation. We need more, not fewer, black organisations; we need black-oriented or black-based youth camps, centres, welfare organisations, etc. For the new black this is a preparatory stage. The means are not now available to enter the final road. Our task is therefore to prepare for 10, 15, and 40 years. The only question now is whether black people are made of such stuff as histories are made of, and black people must answer that question in the presence of the world and in the presence of the black living, the black dead and the black unborn.

Statement of the ANC
(Statement by Mr Mzwandile Piliso, Member of the
National Executive of the African National Congress
of South Africa, to the United Nations Special Committee
On Apartheid on March 27, 1974, and circulated by the
UN Unit on Apartheid)

It is an honour and a great privilege for me that today, deputising for our Acting President, Mr Oliver Tambo, I address this Special Committee with a right to participate fully in your deliberations, not as a petitioner but recognised by the United Nations as an authentic representative of the aspirations of my people. Our presence here is an eloquent acknowledgement of the work this Committee has and is still doing. We salute the dedication of the men and women who serve in it. We are aware of the difficulties that lie ahead for, unfortunately, the interests of mankind do not as yet coincide. There are still those who reap benefits from the suffering of our people.

The history of our country, South Africa, since our people laid down their arms at the end of last century, has been marked by brutal massacres, each time a revolutionary situation appears to exist, in an attempt to frighten off our people and to delay the development of militant struggle. The massacres at Sharpeville and at Carltonville were in line with this development. They will not be the last as long as the status quo is maintained in South Africa. We recognise our responsibility to our people and the world to change that system.

Genocide in South Africa is not confined to these occasional shootings. There are the judicial murders which are committed every year; the political detainees who die under interrogation; the hundreds of thousands of black children who die before they are five years old; the thousands of black people who die of dietary deficiency diseases in a country that feeds skimmed milk to the pigs and that has the highest profit margins in the world for the local and foreign investor.

Our struggle has been long and difficult and we have attempted to show our rulers that it was possible for us all, black and white, to live together in harmony and in peace. In the process some of the best sons of our land have been martyred. Today, faced with the growing intransigence of the racists, our mission still remains unambiguous, the seizure of political power using all available means to rid our country of the scourge of apartheid and to set up a new order where freedom, happiness and peace will reign.

A common struggle for freedom

We believe that the struggle of the oppressed peoples of South Africa is the main guarantee for their freedom. We recognise also the fact that our victories are made possible in part by the significant changes in the world balance of forces. Thus we appreciate the inspiring support rendered to the liberation movement by all peace and freedom-loving peoples within and outside of the United Nations. We attach great significance to the unswerving support and assistance rendered by our African brothers through the OAU, the socialist countries, the Scandinavian countries, some countries of Asia and others.

We would like to emphasise that our struggle is a common struggle. It is a struggle against apartheid, colonialism and imperialism. All those who stand on our side against Vorster do so because we are so right and Vorster is so wrong. Thus people should support us not only because they think apartheid is inhuman and appalling, but above all because apartheid is a crime and a threat to the peace and security of mankind. And those who are involved in the struggle against this system will then cease to be looked upon as victims who need mercy and pity but as nation builders and fighters for a noble and just cause.

We would like to appeal to those countries which, being members of the United Nations, are the main supporters of the South African regime to see reason and join the majority of mankind in condemning apartheid in practical terms and giving direct support to the liberation movement.

We see the success of the national liberation movement not only in the context of countering the fallacy of racism and of the assertion of the position of the black man in world affairs but also in the promotion of the spirit of co-operation and understanding universally.

Supporters of racist South Africa

We believe that it is the bounden duty of mankind as a whole to give a fitting rebuff to the machinations of the South African racists and of the United Nations to lead that onslaught. We are aware that whilst the present composition of the world body should be decisively in favour of the oppressed peoples, racist South Africa still has few but powerful supporters.

It would have been impossible for countries like South Africa and Portugal to so tenaciously hold to their colonial rule if it were not for the fact that they are assured of support by the major powers of the West, who have tried to shield the South African regime from the scathing attacks of the nations of the world, who have resisted and undermined all efforts directed towards effective international action and who have continued to pour arms into South Africa.

The United Nations has passed an impressive list of resolutions on South Africa over the years. Unfortunately, it lacks the instruments for enforcing implementation. We notice with great disturbance the rate at which trade with South Africa is growing each year in spite of United Nations resolutions calling for sanctions against South Africa. We are alarmed that so many Member States of the United Nations still continue to invest in apartheid. The irony of the situation is that this expansion in the volume of investments and trade is coupled with an astronomical rise in the defence budget each year, an increase which is only matched in its rate of growth by the ruthless oppression and grinding poverty to which my people are subjected.

We have warned in the past that by supporting South Africa, the West was building a monster they may not be able to control. And we have repeatedly pointed out that military intervention would neither be new nor accidental to the South African regime because it is consistent with the interventionist and expansionist policy of the racist regime. South Africa sent mercenaries during the intervention in the Congo. Her forces are even today fighting in Angola, Mozambique and Zimbabwe with camps spreading to the banks of the Zambesi River, thus threatening the sovereignty of Zambia. And South African forces are occupying Namibia in violation of United Nations resolutions and in defiance of the United Nations Council for Namibia.

Further fascist measures

Inside South Africa, the apartheid regime continues to foist upon the will of the international community a leadership which it believes has been chizzled with the hammer and anvil of apartheid – a leadership that must comply with the wishes of the Vorster regime – men who are expected to render the balkanisation of our country workable. I refer to the Bantustans. Today, the Bantustan policy remains the fraud it was when it was first mooted. It can never succeed. The real leaders of the oppressed black masses are incarcerated on Robben Island.

Recently, the South African regime has passed further fascist measures relating to the financing of public organisations, to the right of assembly and to the strengthening of the period of military service. These are, in fact, meant as an answer to the rising mobilisation of the oppressed peoples inside the country. The police have voiced suspicion that they might not have succeeded in trapping all ANC men working underground and militarily trained. They have failed to arrest any so-called "ring-leaders" in the waves of strikes since three years ago at least. The attempt to cripple public organisations inside the country, like the South African Students Organization, the Black Peoples' Convention, the

Black Community Programme, etc., by banning their leader-ship, has so far failed. The police are no longer able to control student actions.

We believe that this process is irreversible. The sinister murders that the South African regime is committing outside its borders, far from intimidating our people, will in fact increase their anger and vigilance and inspire them to greater heights of sacrifice.

Action by the United Nations

We of the ANC have watched with great interest develop-ments at the United Nations. We were inspired by the rejection of the credentials of the South African delegation during the last General Assembly. We are aware of the legal difficulties such action entails. But the expulsion of South Africa from the United Nations and all its agencies remains part of our call for the complete isolation of the racist regime.

I have already said how much we appreciate the work this Committee is doing. However, we would like to recommend further activation of this work in areas like Latin America where South Africa is opening up new areas of co-operation and investment. Lately, we have also heard that South Africa and Israel have up-graded their diplomatic representations to the ambassadorial level.

We would like to repeat suggestions we have made in the past; namely, that the United Nations:

1.   Expel the Republic of South Africa and Portugal from all its councils and agencies;

2.   Declare its full support for armed struggle for libera-tion against colonialism and racism and also ensure that appropriate agencies of the United Nations assist in dis-seminating the propaganda material from the liberation movements through all its information media;

3.   Call upon all its Member States to give material support to the people's fighting forces;

4.   Use its good offices to see to it that the Geneva Conventions regarding prisoners of war are observed by the colonialist and racist regimes;

5. Ensure that its social and cultural agencies give assistance to the liberation movements to solve the pressing problems of social and cultural welfare, especially those connected with the education of children of the victims of oppression;

6. Urge all Member States without exception to abide by and respect all United Nations decisions and resolutions and to discipline recalcitrant regimes;

7. Press on the campaign for the release of political prisoners;

8. Mobilise support and assistance for countries bordering the still unliberated territories.

This is the challenge we must place before the United Nations. It is a loud cry from the heart of Namibia where innocent people are subjected to floggings, where leaders are gagged and shoved into prison. It is a loud cry from our comrades-in-arms in Zimbabwe, Mozambique and Angola. It is also a loud cry from the State of Guinea-Bissau.

We of the African National Congress shall spare no effort in our endeavour to eliminate racism, colonialism and imperialism.

The ANC stands with the rest of Africa in support of the OAU on the question of the Middle East. The position was stated clearly by President Gowon during the twenty-eighth session of the General Assembly. The oil embargo dealt a blow on apartheid South Africa. Such acts of solidarity are very meaningful to us. They should, however be intensified.

Appendix 3
Statement of the PAC
(Statement by Mr Potlako Leballo, Acting
President of the Pan Africanist Congress of
Azania, to the United Nations Special Committee
on Apartheid on May 27, 1974, and circulated
by the UN Unit on Apartheid)

When the international community thinks of the political situation in Azania, what looms high in its imagination is the utterly brutal killing of the men, women and children at Sharpeville, Langa, Evaton, Van der Byl Park, Bojhelong, Johannesburg, Durban and Pretoria, on March 21, 1960. Some people think of the political turmoil that led to a financial crisis, loss of profits and the shooting of Prime Minister Verwoard by a desperate white businessman. Others think of apartheid of race prejudice and race discrimination, and of racist gestapo police brutalities, and other horrible inhuman by-products of the fascist dictatorship in that country.

But the oppressed people of Azania think of the revolutionary campaign; of positive action for the abolition of the obnoxious Pass Laws; of the greatest political march in our history that brought the city of Cape Town and the racist white parliament to a standstill nine days after the brutal massacres, when political bankruptcy considered our people to be in disarray. They remember the martyrs of those hectic epic days in our history with national pride, and look forward to the annual occasion to re-dedicate themselves anew to the struggle for which the heroes of Sharpeville and Langa sacrificed their lives.

In the names of the martyrs and heroes of Sharpeville and Langa; on behalf of their dependants; in the name of the African people of Azania; on behalf of the Pan Africanist Congress of Azania, which mobilised the people and organised the revolutionary campaign of positive action that led to the brutal police killings; and in the name of Mangaliso Sobukwe, President and leader of the Pan Africanist Congress of Azania,

149

who launched and led that epic campaign, and is still held to ransom "at the point of the gun" in a small, dusty village outside Kimberley — I take this opprotunity which the Special Committee on Apartheid has afforded me to be present here, to join hands in paying tribute to its work of exposing the evil practices of race prejudice and race antagonism in a racist South Africa and to seek as much as possible to isolate the evil regime and its representatives wherever they may be in the world.

I must also pay tribute to the untiring work the Committee and its illustrious Chairman are doing to try to dissuade racist South Africa's trading partners and their active supporters, from their harmful activities in the service of white supremacy and foreign exploitation of the labour of our people and the material resources of our land. As a result of the work of the Special Committee on Apartheid and other United Nations agencies, the plight of our people and their physical and spiritual disabilities are known the world over. Our national liberation movement is gaining moral and material support from the peace-loving peoples of the entire world. Mr. Chairman, racism and capitalism are a crime against humanity and must be eradicated.

People will liberate themselves

Our gathering here today will not bring back the lives that were brutally brought to an end by the fascists' hail of bullets that were fired indiscriminately at our people fourteen years ago. Who will judge the guilty? Who will avenge the dead? Who will stand up for those who are languishing in Vorster's prisons and concentration camps today? What about those who are being persecuted, brutalised and assassinated today?

As we speak here today, two young men in the prime of their lives, have recently been assassinated by parcel bombs; Abraham Tiro, student leader and President of the South African Student Movement and John Dube, Deputy Representative of the fraternal African National Congress. The South African racist regime is guilty of murdering these two sons of Africa in a cold-blooded manner and without justification whatsoever. These are blood debts that must be repaid in blood.

Our people in the country have awakened to the fact that the struggle for national liberation is their struggle and they alone must liberate themselves. At first they looked to the West, especially Great Britain, for salvation and found they were gravely mistaken. Western capitalism is a system of slavery, and no slave state in the world has ever voluntarily undertaken to emancipate its slaves. Invariably all these states provide for the thorough exploitation of the slaves. Our people have no desire to improve their slave position in the country. They are engaged in overthrowing that slavery outright.

Next, they looked to the "humanity" of the white racist government for human rights and found that they were deluding themselves. They asked for bread and were promised stones. The fraudulent Bantustan policy is not going to lead them to any freedom at all. The people of the Transkei Bantustan have already had more than ten years of practical experience in the workings of that totally fraudulent system and their worst fears have been confirmed. There is nothing to indicate that under it their conditions of life are ever likely to change for the better. Rather they have deteriorated and continue to deteriorate to the point of degeneration. But no nation can be starved to extinction.

When the racist regime banned the organisations of the people in 1960, it believed that it would thus silence all opposition and stifle all determined resistance. By the early seventies the situation had completely changed. Two things became absolutely apparent. The African people began to place major trust in their ability to do things for themselves instead of waiting for someone they don't know, to come around and pull them out of their predicament. Secondly, they saw the imperative need to close their ranks and to seek out of history how to change social development; they decided to make the historical lessons increasingly available to all the

151

oppressed and exploited people in that country.

As a result, we find close solidarity among the oppressed people whom successive racist regimes have tried to separate by race and colour in order to divide and alienate one from the other. That is a situation of the past now. Only the stooge Bantustan Chiefs, puppets and a dead wood of cowards, enter into any form of "dialogue" with the racist regime today. The unity of the oppressed is gaining momentum day by day and this is clearly evident in the Black organisations that are springing up all over the country, in the students' movements and in the workers' movements. The racist government believes it can stem the tide by gagging the leaders of these movements.or, as we have seen recently, by political assassination. But it is too late in the day for it to hope for miracles by such means. As the regime becomes more and more desperate, it cannot avoid alienating itself more and more from the people, both black and white.

In less than a month, the racist white voters are going into several elections in South Africa to give the fascist Broeder-bond government a new mandate. Our people are forever aware of the implications of any white general election in that country. They have not, and will not, ever consider themselves defeated by the white oppressors. Their forefathers submitted to a superior armed aggression, but they cannot remain a conquered people forever. They will not be daunted by the bullets or bayonets of the enemy, or the prospect of probable capture, torture and murder. Their minds are made up. They have accepted the call to battle, as the martyrs and heroes of Sharpeville and Langa did, but this time they have not responded with their bare hands.

The factors of war in that political situation are that men, women and children have gone to war with primitive weapons against a ruthless enemy that uses bombs and bullets and napalm and poison gas against them, at will. They have gone to war, not because they want to die, but because, that way, they will die a noble death. They are being forced to fight and to die even if they are afraid to fight or to die. War is cruel. But so is hunger and poverty. Slavery is much more cruel, and anyone who can stand the cruelty for as long as we have — for over three hundred years — since 1652 — must be in an even better position to stand the cruelty of war. We owe it to the martyrs of Sharpeville, Langa and other battlefields.

Sharpeville — a turning point

We must remember that Sharpeville was the greatest turning point in our history of resistance to tyranny where non-violence was buried. It was the beginning of a new era of armed struggle. For the first time, at Sharpeville, the people of Azania challenged the racist government by putting forward an alternative government of a non-racialist socialist democracy under the banner of African Nationalism and Pan Africanism. The Pan Africanist Congress of Azania demanded the downfall of that tyrannical regime and without ceremony. Never before had any mass struggle and its attendant crisis rocked the country to its very foundations. For the first time in the racist set-up, the regime declared a state of emergency out of a purely political crisis. For the first time in the history of that country, the fascist gestapo-like police were forced to announce the suspension of the pass laws for men because of the political crisis.

Prime Minister Verwoerd was shot in the head, the first time that such an incident had taken place since the formation of the Union of South Africa. Paul Sauer, who acted as Prime Minister while Verwoerd was struggleing for his life in hospital, made his famous Humansdorp speech, in which he warned and urged the white people to consider honestly and earnestly the whole approach to the situation of the African people in the country. He warned, "South Africa will never be the same again after Sharpeville."

Even the racist government press published comments in its editorials and correspondence columns, asking for a new approach. For the first time, it considered Africans as people and its reporters interviewed them - even on the streets - and

153

published what they said. In the face of the determined political struggle and crisis, apartheid became a lost cause without cry or advocate, and ceased to be mentioned in public: 400,000 white settlers fled the country; the economy collapsed and the end was in sight. Had the United States imperialism not intervened with over 200 million dollars to save the tottering racist regime, the situation would have been different today. Even Verwoerd rose from his sick bed and talked of divine providence having saved him from death to continue to lead the so-called chosen race of white people to the era of peace and abundance. But this was not the end.

This is not to say that Sharpeville occurred in isolation or dropped out of the blue sky. The history of Sharpeville is unsurpassed, nor can its history be falsified by anyone. The Pan Africanist Congress had challenged the regime in a contest for political power. President Mangaliso Sobukwe who led the campaign, publicly declared that we were taking the first step that would lead to independence and the unification of the African continent. He declared: "Let the world take note, in this phase of the struggle, our energies and forces are directed against a set-up; against a concept and a myth, the demi-god of white supremacy." The Sharpeville massacre and other shootings took place to hide the success of that historic campaign and to snatch the fruits of victory from the people who earned it, the broad masses of our people who answered the call to positive action.

It has been clearly and authoritatively pointed out that without the support of its western trading partners and capital investors, racism would not survive on the African continent. This was shown in 1960 and 1961. Certain members of this United Nations Organization came to the rescue of South Africa and have never looked back. But, we are aware and have studied the full implications of the tentacles of the imperialist global strategy of the mercenary movement which has been unleashed upon oppressed peoples and the nations of the world.

Kill or be killed

Mr Chairman, we earnestly appeal to the Member States of the international community to isolate this apartheid regime, economically, politically, socially and militarily. We also direct our appeal to the Member States of this august body to give assistance to the liberation movement for a total overthrow of this apartheid regime.

The racist regime has stated with arrogance to us that we shall attain our freedom in South Africa over their dead bodies. Therefore, there can be no two ways in this contest of power. Our position is clear — KILL OR BE KILLED. No doubt we shall have to walk over their dead bodies if we are to achieve our meaningful freedom in an armed struggle against these racists. We have no fear of death whatsoever. We have nothing to lose, but the Continent of Africa to regain.

LONG LIVE THE AFRICAN REVOLUTION!

Appendix 4
Statement of the Unity Movement

(Soweto: The Call to Arms, issued by V.K. Scrape Ntshona of the Unity Movement of South Africa, June 1976, Since this is a 20 page statement, it has had to be abridged here for reasons of space.)

. . . After the founding of the Union of South Africa in 1910, the government policy of segregation did not end with the separation between Africans, Coloured and Asians, who constitute the black oppressed majority. When the (Boer) Nationalist Government acceded to power in 1948 it widened and extended the policy of segregation (apartheid) to ethnic divisions among the African section by a process of retribalisation in the urban areas to ensure a steady supply of cheap black labour to South Africa's industry. Although all of the blacks suffered disenfranchisement, the vertical separation, unequal treatment and political suppression of the sections below the horizontal colour bar produced suspicion and hostility among the different groups and made it difficult to achieve a wide-based unity among them in the political struggle.

On 18th June the Theron Commission, appointed by the government in 1973 to review the position of the Coloured people in South African society, published its report which recommended fundamental changes in Government policy for Coloured people such as the repeal of amendment of the Mixed Marriage Act, the 'Immorality' (sex across the colour line) Act, the Group Areas Act (setting aside certain areas for the sole occupation of different races), the Industrial Conciliation Act, as well as changing race classification methods and the election of Coloured members of parliament. The government, needless to say, rejected the fundamental changes proposed, but accepted the proposals for the removal or relaxation of much of the less crucial apartheid for Coloureds in order to try and further divide and weaken the liberation movement. The efforts in recent years of SASO which expanded the base of the independent students' organisations to include all sections in the black consciousness movement, as well as the current protest action by the Coloured and African students should go some way towards the establishment of a united struggle of the oppressed people. Coloured young men between the ages of 18 and 27 are compelled by law to attend conscription centres where they are taught discipline and trade skills so as to replace African labour which by government policy is being phased out of the Cape Town Western Province of South Africa. This has created deep divisions between Africans and Coloureds.

The Coloured population of the sprawling townships of Athlone and Bonteheuvel in the Western Cape has since extended its political protest dramatically. Thousands of school pupils and young workers took to the streets in militant demonstrations calling for 'power for the people' and the ending of apartheid. They attacked government property and fought running battles with the police who tried to break up the demonstrations. The police headed off several hundred schoolchildren who were marching towards the neighbouring township of Langa for a joint demonstration of Coloured and African children. Subsequently Coloured and African children converged on the centre for a mass protest which defied police efforts to disperse it. It must now be clear to the government that its policy of divide and rule among the blacks is bound to fail. The Coloureds who have been racially separated from Africans and designated 'an appendage of the Whites' have now signified in unmistakable terms that they have always formed a constituent part of the resistance movement.

Although the flashpoint in Soweto was reached over the 'Afrikaans' language issue, the history of student struggle goes back nearly ten years. In 1969 a group of students from the black University Colleges formed the South African students' Organisation (SASO). One of its early decisions was to disaffiliate black (African, Coloured and Asian) students from the mainly white National Union of South African

Students (NUSAS) and establish an independent body. They recognised that while NUSAS fought for academic freedom and equality for all students, it could only be limited in its activity to the academic field and to general support for the amelioration of the condition of blacks in South African society. They (SASO) on the other hand realised that academic freedom could not be brought about without a radical change in South African society to establish black rule. They saw the black masses as their area of primary responsibility and they went into action with a drive against illiteracy and anti-poverty programmes in the black areas as the practical part of their policy of involvement in the movement for political change. The early 70s saw a lot of action against Government policies in the black university campuses of Natal, the North Western Cape and Fort Hare. In the pursuit of its goal of student participation in the liberation movement, SASO was instrumental in the formation of the Black People's Convention (BPC), a loose political federation of workers' organisations.

SASO extended its activities to secondary schools with the formation of the South African Students' Movement (SASM) which proceeded to form units in various secondary schools, particularly in Soweto. SASM opposed the rigid application of the policy of inferior education, co-ordinated their efforts with SASO, and generally supported the fight for freedom. In April 1976, two units of the SASM from two secondary schools were arrested by the Special Branch police and committed for trial under the Terrorism Act. The treason trial of leading members of SASO under the Terrorism Act was still in progress when the Soweto uprising took place.

Early this year the Department of Bantu Education enforced a ruling which it had made in 1955 that half of the subjects in the curriculum should be taught in English and the other in Afrikaans, both of them the official languages of the rulers. It further stipulated that Mathematics, Science and Social Studies would be the subjects to be taught in Afrikaans. Teachers, pupils and parents all opposed this move on the grounds that both teachers and pupils were more pro-

ficient in English and there was a shortage of Afrikaans —
qualified teachers. Progress in education would be painfully
slow, resulting in a further lowering of the already inferior
educational standards for blacks. Moreover, Afrikaans was
the language of the vicious Afrikaner government, and the
elevation of this local and poorly developed language to a
position of parity with the 'international' language of English
was regarded as a vindictive and punitive measure against
blacks ...

. . . The present generation of students has gone through
school and university with a strong sense of grievance against
a harsh and desperate authority and acute intellectual, social
and cultural deprivation. Having been brought up in the bleak
existence and degrading poverty of semi-rural areas and the
squalor of urban ghettoes they shared the frustration and
bitterness that are their parents' lot. They have always had
to fight for survival against deliberately imposed disabilities
and for the opportunities to uplift themselves by their own
bootstraps.

Armed with a theoretical analysis and a higher social consciousness they forged a policy and programme for long term
resistance to a baneful ruling class. In the first phase of their
strategy they politicised and raised the level of social awareness of the students in the campuses in preparation for their
revolt against intellecutal impoverishment and the intolerable
conditions in their academic institutions. The next phase took
the practical form of establishing links with the community
in order to take part in the day-to-day activities of the people.
In their baptism of fire the students stood alongside the
workers at the barricades in the inevitable confrontation with
the police which followed and became an integral part of the
resistance movement. With uncharacteristic sagacity they
helped to found the BPC which would form an organisational
link between students and workers and which they could join
after leaving University. In the high schools they formed
SASM for the younger pupils to take part in their fight. The
collapse of Portuguese imperialism in Mozambique and

Angola raised the expectations of the militant students sharply and they stepped up their action in the schools over the Afrikaans language issue. . .

Soweto has now been developed into a power base for the resistance movement, a kind of 'no go' area which police fear to enter at night. Many black policemen who reside there have had their homes attacked, and have now fled the area. They are reluctant to take part in police operations in Soweto even during daytime lest they are recognised and marked for reprisals. The young political movement is increasing its control over the political life of Soweto. It plans the workers' industrial action which has had such a telling effect on the economy. Industrialists now admit that the strikes have caused falling productivity and lower profitability in some enterprises. . .

. . . The South African economy, which is built on the explosive commodity of discontented black labour, is vulnerable to organised and stiffening black resistance, albeit intermittent. Dependent as it is for its survival on foreign capital which requires a stable political climate, the government is extremely sensitive and reacts with utmost severity against black unrest.

When industrial action becomes widespread such as was the case between 1973 and 1975 when literally hundreds of thousands of black workers went on strike throughout the country against low wages and increased living costs, the economy was seriously disrupted and the employers were forced to make wage concessions. The government was unable to stop the wave of strikes which are illegal for black workers in South Africa. Its ability to control the black work force and maintain a favourable climate for foreign investment had been compromised and the workers who had flexed their muscles and realised their potential would, no doubt, use their tremendous power to defend themselves and possibly go on to challenge state power in the future.

The economy has gone into a deep recession in the past few months. In his last Budget, the Minister of Finance,

Senator O. Horwoed, stated that there was 'every reason to expect that the deficit on current account will be substantially lower in 1976 than in 1975. . . . a deficit of this order should be covered by a normal inflow of (foreign) capital'. At the end of 1974 when the price of gold, the main pillar of the economy, was at its peak, he had predicted an average of US $200 an ounce. On the basis of these miscalculations and misplaced optimism, the government boosted 'armaments' expenditure to a high level record and went ahead stockpiling strategic materials and massive capital-intensive projects such as the nuclear reactor. The result was that inflation soared and the amount of imports nearly trebled in three years. The price of gold plummeted to $106 and the balance of payments deficit soared to a record R1,953 million by the end of June 1976, and is likely to run at an estimated average of R120 million a month in the next few months. The share of foreign capital in domestic investment increased by 4% in 1975 -76, and although the net inflow of foreign capital for 1975—76 was R1,619 million, in the June 1976 quarter the net inflow of foreign funds was apparently nil. The reserves fell R350 million from R1,100 million to R750 million in the four months ending June 1976. The hope for staving off a second devaluation of the Rand in the next twelve months lies in the prospect of a loan from European countries and a further drawing from the International Monetary Fund.

In the rising inflation with increased prices of basic commodities, the hardest hit section of the population is the poorly paid black worker. African unemployment has increased with sizeable redundancies in the motor and other manufacturing industries. At a rising rate of 20,000 every month the number of unemployed Africans may have exceeded the 2 million mark of 20% of the economically active Africans according to an estimate prepared by Charles Simkins a researcher at the University of Cape Town. The government does not keep official statistics on African unemployment. Cutbacks in spending on black education and expenditure on urban townships have been reported. Some of the most powerful employer organisations have adopted the strategy of meting out punishments to workers who step out of line while industry makes strenuous efforts to increase or at least hold diminishing profits. To break the workers' strike the employers refused to pay workers who stayed at home. In several factories restiveness has been met by instant dismissal of the entire work force followed by selective re-hirings; those who promise to remain docile are signed on again, while alleged 'agitators' do not get their jobs back. Inevitably, the educated workers become the first to be victimised. Black workers have no trade unions to represent them and the government and business management persist in refusing recognition to the few trade unions which are in the process of formation.

When the economy took a sharp downturn in 1975 after the massive strikes and was heading for devaluation there was considerable anxiety in ruling circles about the future supply to the mining industry of migrant labour from Mozambique after the victory of the anti-imperialist revolution. As a result the government accelerated its plans for granting independence to its major labour reservoir, the Transkei, in order to increase the flow of indigenous labour to the mines. Additional land concessions were made to the Transkei at the expense of the less important Ciskei and legislation was rushed through parliament to ensure the continuation after independence of South Africa's annual subsidy to the Transkei of 75% of that Bantustan's yearly budget. Powers of repression under the law were ceded to the Bantustan to enable its leaders to put down all opposition to the fraud of independence. The government also compelled the Bantustan to agree to the *quid pro quo* of accepting all Africans originating or descended from the Transkei but residing and working outside it as citizens of the Bantustan. This would have the diabolical effect of making urban Africans foreigners in South Africa. They would be able to obtain employment in the cities only as migrant workers staying in hostels without their families. The migratory labour system is now being extended in South Africa as one of the instruments for reducing the unit cost of labour and for maximising profits. Through this system local authorities and the government are relieved of the obligation to expend capital on social services for workers such as housing and services, health, education and other amenities. . .

. . . The oppressed people have now found new strength and they know that with a correct political strategy and a united revolutionary organisation the struggle can be extended to prepare for the seizure of power. A greater unity in struggle among all black people has been brought into sharper focus, strengthening the social forces which are working for radical change. This has been made possible by the spectacular success of the political strategy of the student movement. In the past these learned young men condescended from their theoretical ivory towers to tell the workers how to conduct the political struggle through their writings and lectures delivered in the conferences which were an important feature of the liberation movement before the sixties and which the workers never attended. SASO did not appraoch the workers as teachers. They fought for change inside the universities and schools and extended their action to involvement with the people in the community. In this way they established an area of common interest, a common destiny with similar goals for workers and students. This convincing approach of commitment, action and identity secured the mass response of the workers in support of the militant students. . .

. . . The students could not be expected to raise the level of struggle much more than the gigantic efforts they have made so far. No one realises the limitations of the black consciousness movement more than the students themselves. Although they are capable of making a theoretical analysis of social problems, the correctness and validity of such an analysis can only be determined by testing it in actual practice. Since student life lasts only a short number of years in which students are preoccupied with their academic pursuits, they do not gain sufficient experience and will not have enough time to test their ideas in the heat of battle. The number of students is small compared with workers and the academic institution is less crucial than industry in South African capitalist society. The social weight of the students is therefore much smaller than that of the workers on whom they must lean and depend. The students realise that they cannot change their academic institutions alone since these are a reflection and form a small part of existing society. Many students succumb to the temptations of a comfortable life when they leave university and they lose their connection with the revolutionary current. This happened frequently in the past because there was no active political organisation to absorb them. Action without theory is inadequate to solve the task of national liberation from oppression and economic exploitation, and the participation of the students is essential in the conditions of South Africa for their own benefit and in the higher interest of emancipation for the blacks. Revolution is a conscious process for the achievement of precise goals with a clear strategy and programme.

To take the struggle further now requires a permanent revolutionary vanguard organisation to co-ordinate and unify the various sections — students, industrial workers, the countryside - of the population in revolt and ensure continuation and the achievement of its goals. Only such an organisation, formed expressly for defending the interests of workers and peasants and for taking over political and economic power from the white minority to establish a non-racial democracy can perform this task. The ruling minority will not voluntarily relinquish its absolute power and wealth or even share power with the black masses whose exploited labour produces that wealth and power. Real freedom for the blacks will be attained when they forcibly take public ownership and control of the land and the economy. A broadly based national liberation Front including all sections of the oppressed people appears to be the most appropriate vehicle for the liberation movement. Several liberation movements exist, divided by history and not by widely separated levels of political consciousness. The political spectrum of the Front will be understandably wide, taking in the least developed to the most politically advanced members. The Front can unite all these elements on the basis of a political programme for national liberation as a first step. The liberation struggle can only be taken on its upper goals by a revolutionary vanguard organisation within, formed out of and leading the Front politically. . .

Appendix 5
Ways and Means of Counteracting South African Propaganda
(issued by the Centre Against Apartheid, Department of Political and Security Council Affairs, United Nations, New York, June 1976)

Because of the growing opposition to racism in world public opinion, the Pretoria regime has found it increasingly difficult to win public support. It is conducting its propaganda in a hostile world, while public opinion is favourable to the opponents of apartheid

The effectiveness of the South African propaganda should not be exaggerated. Even the Pretoria regime now recognises that apartheid is an unsaleable commodity in the world market. That is why the emphasis is on trying to persuade the world that racial discrimination is being removed in South Africa, that sanctions against South Africa are harmful and that liberation movements should not be supported.

However, recent experience shows that it is dangerous to ignore South African propaganda. Especially when it is supported by Western Governments or powerful financial interests, and when it is able to distort the issues it can create confusion among public opinion.

The United Nations Special Committee against apartheid has always regarded the dissemination of information as an adjunct to action to isolate the South African regime and to assist the liberation movements — rather than as a mere exercise in publicising facts on the inhumanity of apartheid, though such factual information is necessary. The purpose of information is to mobilise world public support for the implementation of United Nations resolutions and to promote assistance to the liberation movements. It is to encourage public opinion in the Western countries which collaborate with the South African regime to struggle against such collaboration by their governments and corporations.

It might be emphasised, at the outset, that there is no better propaganda than action itself. Campaigns against collaboration with South Africa, boycotts of racist South

African sports teams, and decisions of international organisations, such as the exclusion of the South African delegation from the United Nations General Assembly, have made millions in South Africa and the rest of the world aware of the problem of apartheid. Even when such campaigns were resisted by powerful interests, the result was a controversy which attracted national and international attention. Controversy is preferable to apathy, since the main interest of the South African regime is to make the world ignore apartheid and forget the leaders in prison and their sacred cause.

In planning an expansion of information activity in support of liberation in South Africa, there should be constant co-operation among all forces opposed to apartheid: the United Nations; the specialised agencies such as UNESCO, ILO, WHO and FAO; the OAU; the Non-aligned Movement; the Arab League; Member States; trade unions, churches and non-governmental organisations; information media; and, above all, the liberation movements.

The information campaign should be directed toward the following ends:

(a) constantly expose the inhumanity of apartheid, and show that apartheid is not merely racial discrimination but the oppression and exploitation of the great majority of the people, and a crime against humanity;

(b) counteract, with facts, the propaganda regarding reforms within apartheid, and stress that there can be no compromise on the total eradication of apartheid and the liberation of South Africa;

(c) publicise and denounce all collaboration with South Africa by governments, economic and financial interests and others;

(d) fight all manoeuvres and propaganda by the South African regime to divide African and other States, and stress that any compromise with apartheid is a betrayal of the principles of the United Nations and OAU;

(e) counteract all propaganda designed to treat the problem of apartheid according to "cold war" thinking and emphasise the right of the liberation movements to seek and receive assistance from all sources in their legitimate struggle; and

(f) denounce all propaganda in favour of military links with South Africa and make it clear that any country entering into a formal or informal military alliance with the racist regime will face the hostility of the overwhelming majority of the States and peoples of the world.

The campaign should clearly isolate and define the allies of the South African regime and instruments of its propaganda. They include, in particular, powerful business interests in Western countries; a number of members of legislatures and other influential persons who are connected with such business interests; several military officers who are insensitive to racism and spread South African "cold war" propaganda; and a number of newspapers directly or indirectly connected with South Africa.

They form the lobbies for South Africa in various Western countries. A study of these racist lobbies should be urgently undertaken, and an international campaign launched against them.

It has already been emphasised that the United Nations is only one of the agencies playing a role in the dissemination of information against apartheid.

Within the United Nations, the decision to launch an information effort and the creation of the Unit on Apartheid (now Centre against Apartheid) has been an important contribution to the struggle against apartheid. The Centre has performed its task with dedication, despite its limited resources, and deserves the commendation it has received from the Special Committee, the liberation movements and other solidarity movements.

Attention will need to be given to expanding its work. The

Special Committee will soon consider concrete proposals for this purpose. At this stage, it may be appropriate to suggest a few needs:

(a) The Centre should be provided the necessary resources to produce more attractive publications for mass distribution in all languages.

(b) It should produce publications for special groups and for specific campaigns against apartheid.

(c) It should also be provided resources for production of audio-visual materials.

(d) Governments should be requested to help the Centre by redisseminating its material widely through national information media.

(e) The staff of the Centre should be enabled to visit capitals to promote information campaigns.

While the Centre does play an important role, and can play a greater role, it cannot be expected to take responsibility for all aspects of the information campaign indicated above.

For the exposure of and the struggle against the allies of the South African regime, the initiative will need to be taken by political bodies – the Special Committee against Apartheid the liberation movements, the OAU and the solidarity and anti-apartheid movements. Consultations among these bodies is essential in order to plan co-ordinated activity against the disseminators of the poisonous propaganda of the apartheid regime and the profiters from the oppression of the South African people.

Appendix 6
FESTAC REPORT ON MASS MEDIA
SECOND WORLD BLACK AND AFRICAN FESTIVAL OF
ARTS AND CULTURE (FESTAC)
The Colloquium Division, January/February 1977
Lagos, Nigeria

Working Group 5 Report
SUB-THEME: BLACK CIVILISATION AND MASS MEDIA

Chairmen: Mr E. Jengo   (Tanzania)
              Professor A.E. Opubor   (Nigeria)
              Professor P.B. Camara   (Guinea)

Rapporteur: Mr C.C. Chimutengwende (Zimbabwe)

In all, fifteen papers were presented in Working Group Five on the sub-theme BLACK CIVILISATION AND MASS MEDIA. Eleven of the fifteen authors briefly summarised their papers and answered questions on them. The other four papers were circulated as background information for the discussions.

The papers and discussions dealt with various aspects of mass communication media as follows:—

1.   The importance and power of the media in transmitting cultural, political and educational messages;
2.   Traditional and modern forms of communication;
3.   Technology and the media;
4.   Neo-colonialism and the political and cultural outlook of the media in Africa;
5.   Information work and the liberation movement; and
6.   The media in the social, cultural and economic development process.

The term mass media was understood as covering the press, radio, television, cinema and all other large-scale information media. Their content is public and can reach vast audiences in a short space of time.

It was stressed that mass communication was essential to every nation trying to modernise itself and to every movement trying to spearhead the struggle for liberation and the democratisation of society.

The media can effectively help to maintain contact and understanding between the government and the people, between rural areas and the cities, and among nations. Nationally, the media are an important integrative agency. They are a powerful force as an educator, agitator, mobiliser, motivator and entertainer. Their power can be great but immeasurable. They can create a feeling of involvement and participation. It is through them that the national agenda of the day is presented to the nation. They are a national forum for the continuous debate which is necessary in every country, on issues and problems. No developing country therefore, serious about its development programme and no country struggling against neo-colonialist social and economic structures can afford mass media which are mainly for commercial purposes and not committed to the national cause.

While it was the general view of the Working Group that inter-personal communication or face-to-face communication was the most effective way of communicating among the people, inter-personal channels of communication themselves are speeded up and fed by the mass media. The two forms of communication are complementary. The traditional methods of communication were almost entirely inter-personal. The main forms were:

Proverbs

Poetry

Theatre, ie indigenous dances and songs

Stories and

Rituals.

It is important that these methods of communicating should be researched into, developed and integrated with the new methods of mass communication. It is by publishing and broadcasting in African languages that one can use proverbs, rituals, stories, etc, and be able to reach more people for the development of the country. What language must be used is a very important question. It partly decides who the media are intended to serve - the elite or the people?

Language being a vehicle for culture and communication, the mass media must be made to give priority to local and not foreign languages which are mainly used by foreigners and the local elite whose culture is more foreign than African. Ignoring African languages which are spoken by the majority of the people means that the media will not be able to transmit the cultural, political and educational messages conducive to a speedy socio-economic development process.

There must be a proper and suitable style and presentation for each medium and its audience clearly defined. This is the role of mass communication research centres which must be created in different universities and be supported by the state. These centres could study and identify all these problems and alternatives for the policy planners of the state concerned with the media and the economic development programme. The journalists and other media workers must be fully trained as one of the national priorities and according to specific national objectives. The press men must be people who understand the material conditions of the people, identify with their aspirations and the struggle against the forces of oppression and under-development.

On the question of technology and the media, it was realised that the media are technological devices for communication. The printing machines, the radio and television sets and equipment are usually imported from abroad. Many African States cannot even afford much of the technology necessary for an up-to-date mass communication system. But the group felt that the problem is not one of not being able to acquire the most sophisticated media technology for the most sophisticated and fastest ways of communication. It is not even a question of which medium is more effective than others. The real problem is what are the actual objectives in our present communication work? What are we doing with the media as an instrument of liberation and development in our countries? What does the development plan say about it? What section of the population in our countries is served by the media? Why? Once our governments and people have sorted out their minds on these questions, we could than move forward to discuss the scientific and technological aspects of mass communication; decide what we need and what we can afford and the best ways of using the media. It is a question of setting our priorities right and being guided by the principle of self-reliance as much as possible.

The Working Group discussed the idea that mass media need an industrial structure of a complex, scientific and technological character, and the relationship between the transfer of ideas and the transfer of technology. It was the general opinion of the group that the less developed countries should make sure that they do not culturally and politically become dominated by the multi-national corporations and the governments of the countries from which they get their technology. At present, the exchange of information and ideas between the former colonial powers and the ex-colonies is one-sided. It is from the developed or the stronger to the less developed or the weaker to the disadvantage of the latter.

Those who dominate the world or society also dominate the dominant media. They are bound to use the media to promote their interests to the disadvantage of the dominated. But people do not change their views and attitudes so easily. In fact the media tend rather to reinforce existing opinions than change them. While the power of the media is recognised, it is also true that they are only one of the factors which influence people. In a society where the media are clearly an instrument of the oppressor, for instance in Cuba before the revolution, they are not able to influence the oppressed to accept their oppression for ever. The Cuban revolution was eventually successful in spite of the negative position of the media, at that point in time. In Zimbabwe and Azania the media are totally opposed to the liberation of the African

173

people. Although the African people largely depend on them for information and entertainment, the overwhelming majority of the Africans in these countries remain faithful to the struggle for liberation. The struggle continues unabated.

Speaker after speaker emphasised the point that the mass media in Africa were introduced as instruments for aiding and consolidating the system of colonialism. The media were seen as one of the sectors which have strongly retained their colonial outlook in most parts of independent Africa. Although the media could be an extremely useful and effective instrument for the total liberation and development of Africa most governments seem to ignore their mobilisation, educational and development potential or at least do not use the media as fully as they should. This is a result of having twisted priorities and having no coherent and comprehensive policy on national development.

The media have never been a neutral element in society. They are not independent agents and cannot be. They operate under the law. They are owned by someone for certain reasons. They are run in accordance with the wishes of the people who own them. They are run by human beings who are members of society and represent certain views and interests like every other individual citizen. The media therefore reflect the political and economic system or philosophy in any country. The dominant media automatically represent the dominant ideas and culture of the ruling centres of power. If they don't, sooner or later there will be an unavoidable clash between the government and the media. The government would win in such a clash unless there was a successful revolution or counter-revolution.

In the post-independence period, another manifestation of imperialism reveals itself in the way the mass media in most parts of Africa are dependent on western sources of information, technology of the multi-national corporations, and their organisational structures and ethics which are a carbon copy of those of the "former" colonial powers. Most of the newspapers are not only versions of the *France Soir*

174

or the *Daily Mirror* of London, but poor imitations of them. The orientation of their content, the pattern of media ownership, the cultural and political outlook of the media staff, all clearly show that the media cannot be agents of liberation, national development and for spreading the authentic culture of the African people unless the media themselves are liberated first. It is because of this colonial outlook and their being a dependent institution that many people nationally and internationally do not take the African media seriously. So they continue to rely on foreign broadcasts and newspapers. (Of course another reason is that the educated elite mostly trained in Western Europe and North America, after having spent years of socialisation abroad, when they come back want to continue to depend on the Western media. Culturally most of them are now westerners.)

Unlike the media situation in other continents, the relationship between the African media and the state has not been properly defined. Because of this situation, very often the journalists are not sure what to, and what not to print or broadcast. Instead of writing a comment on certain issues, they find the safest thing to do is to use the material from foreign news agencies. The idea is to avoid being held responsible for certain opinions and possible innuendoes. For the media to play their proper role effectively, they should be at the service of the majority of the people and not give priority to the aspirations, the struggle and progress of the masses. The music and other cultural programmes or items should be geared to the promotion and development of the people's music and culture.

The information in the media must focus on the need and methods of change. They must identify and expose the relics and machinations of imperialism. They must help the people to raise their consciousness and their level of participation in the decision-making processes of their countries. The media should be made useful instruments of informal education and in literacy campaigns.

On the use of the media in schools, it was strongly argued

that the media were under-utilised except in countries where there is free and compulsory education plus a massive state-directed national literacy campaign. At this stage, therefore, the starting point is one of defining national priorities with clear media objectives and this is a political question which has to be solved first in most countries before any serious progress can be made.

On the question of film distribution, the group was disheartened by the fact that the majority of films shown in cinema houses in many countries of Africa and the Black world deal with non-African realities and when they deal with African and Black life, they tend to trivialise, misrepresent and distort it. This situation is unfortunate, especially in view of the growing number of young talented film makers in Africa and the Black World. The work of these film makers is not generally well known because it does not receive the blessing of the dominant film distribution cartels.

The Group felt that one other important aspect of FESTAC was that it had been able to bring together mass media workers, trainers, researchers, experts and other interested people to share their experiences and exchange ideas on the question of mass media. It was further strongly suggested that resolutions to be passed in the Working Groups should be followed up through the appropriate channels and we must make sure they are not thrown into the usual dustbin of international resolutions. At this point, one participant informed the Working Group about the existence of the African Council on Communication Education which was formed in Nairobi, Kenya, at a Conference in December 1976, of mass communication researchers, trainers and experts from different parts of Africa. It publishes AFRICOM, a bi-lingual newsletter bi-monthly. Both institutions and individuals can qualify for membership. It exists to co-ordinate and encourage communication research, education and the practice of journalism.

The Group agreed that there was an urgent need for such an organisation or institution. It is through their own well-supported research that African States can be helped to employ their mass media effectively. At present, researchers from outside Africa guide much of our media use in Africa.

The Group also stressed the fact that the major problems of Africa were not of Africa alone. Other countries of Asia, the Middle East, Caribbean Islands, South and Central America have similar problems and it is essential for them to co-ordinate their efforts. African states would not be able to achieve real understanding among themselves and other "Third World" countries if the media and the sources of information are controlled or heavily influenced by the former colonial masters, or if the media continued to be run by people who did not identify clearly with African liberation and development.

RECOMMENDATIONS OF WORKING GROUP 5
Sub-Theme: Black Civilisation and Mass Media

Fully aware of the central role of the mass media in the political cultural, scientific, technological and professional development of the African countries and communities of people of African descent;

Conscious of the need to transform the mass media into effective, educational and mobilising instruments in the struggle for liberation and development;

Realising the need for Africa to liberate its media from the tutelage of the international press agencies and to effectively counteract the massive foreign influence of those foreign media opposed to African economic, political and cultural independence and development;

Considering the need to make the mass media accessible to the majority of the population;

In conformity with the recommendations of the Conference of African Ministers of Culture held in Accra in 1975 in connection with the position of the mass media in a dynamic cultural policy, orientated towards the promotion of the true interests of the African peoples; in connection with these objectives, we recommend the following measures:

1. That the OAU draft an elaborate charter for the mass media defining the rights and obligations of the press men;
2. That there be a programme of exchange of journalists between African countries and regular continent-wide conferences of journalists and other media personnel which should include people of African descent outside Africa;
3. That the OAU organise the African national news agencies for the purpose of establishing a Pan-African news agency which would be a machinery for direct exchange of news and programmes between African States, Black communities internationally and thus avoid being dependent on foreign news services;
4. That the OAU should investigate the aims, activities and seriousness of purpose of the recently formed African Council on Communication Education based in Nairobi, with a view to getting support for it as the continent-wide organisation for the promotion and co-ordination of communication research, education and the practice of journalism;
5. That a well-financed and high-powered journal on mass communication research and the media in general in Africa should be established by the OAU and/or UNESCO;
6. That an institute of cinematography should be created in order to promote the African cinema in the field of conception, production and distribution, and for the production and distribution of audio-visual materials;
7. That more attention should be given to the efforts of local scholars, artists, scientists and others in the media than to foreigners and that African governments should

establish more publishing houses with special interest in manuscripts written in local languages; and that the media be made to use African national languages in order to reach more people;

8. That an appropriate institution or organisation be found which will encourage direct contact among Africans, people of African descent, all those struggling for liberation around the world, and encouragement be given for the exchange of audio and video cassettes recorded by local groups and sent by one group or community (say in East Africa) to another (say in the Caribbean or Australia);

9. That training institutions must be made to pay more attention to the needs of rural and non-elite people in their curricula and orientate thair students to acquire expertise in communicating with the non-elite and this may involve training in traditional media and inter-personal communication techniques;

10. That all countries participating in FESTAC undertake to increase the amount of time they spend in their media on information and programmes reflecting the culture and struggles of other Black and African peoples and all those fighting for liberation internationally;

11. That since the liberation movements recognised by the OAU struggling for the freedom of Azania (South Africa), Zimbabwe (Rhodesia), Namibia (South West Africa), Djibouti (Somali Coast) and communities of African descent internationally have to fight against massive, well-financed and well-coordinated propaganda offen-sives of the white racist regimes which they are struggling against, and since this enemy propaganda offensive is both internal and external, it is essential, therefore, that the IFC of FESTAC recommends to the OAU that a high-powered machinery be established to supplement the propaganda work of the liberation movements and the liberation movements could then be left to con-centrate on internal information work, while the new

propaganda machinery of the OAU would concentrate on information and research work for the international community.

Postscript

As this book was going to press The Government of South Africa banned 18 organisations and two black-run newspapers and arrested more than 60 black and white people in a dramatic nationwide police swoop on October 19, 1977. This was the most important political development in South Africa since the 1960 Sharpeville massacres, mass arrests, banishments and restrictions which equally shook and disgusted the international community.

The 18 banned organisations some of which were discussed in Chapter Three of this book are: The Association for the Educational and Cultural Advancement of the African People of South Africa; the Black Parents' Association; The Black People's Convention; The Black Women's Federation; The Border Youth Organisation, also known as the Border Youth Union; The Christian Institute of South Africa; The Eastern Province Youth Organisation, also known as the Eastern Cape Youth Organisation; the Medupe Writers' Association; The Natal Youth Organisation; The National Youth Organisation; The South African Students' Movement; The South African Students' Organisation; The Soweto Students' Representative Council; The Black Community Programmes; The Transvaal Youth Organisation; The Union of Black Journalists; The Western Cape Youth Organisation; The Zimele Trust.

The following are some of the best known people who were detained or restricted during the same period: Kenneth

Rachidi, President of the Black People's Convention; Percy Qoboza, Editor of the *World*; Dr Nthato Motlana, medical doctor and Chairman of the Soweto Committee of 10; D. Lolwane, Leslie Mathabathe, Leonard Mosala, Ellen Khuzwayo, all members of the Committee of 10; Fanyana Mazibuku, Secretary of the Soweto Teachers' Committee which had organised a strike by several hundred black teachers; Jairus Kgokong, an official of the Soweto branch of the Black People's Convention; Father Smangaliso Mkhatshwa, a Soweto churchman; Aggrey Klaaste, news editor of *Weekend World*; Vivian Made, National Director of the Black People's Convention. White liberals opposed to the racist philosophy of apartheid, like Donald Woods, editor of *East London Daily Dispatch*. Dr. B. Naude, a Dutch Reformed Church Minister and founder member of the Christian Institute of South Africa, and three of his colleagues were also banned.

Some of the banned organisations had become extremely popular and influential among black people in South Africa. Some were not directly political and others were very moderate organisations with a multi-racial membership or were working in close collaboration with white liberals, churches and industrialists. Others, like the Simele Trust, were welfare and educational organisations.

The more political movements such as the Black People's Convention (BPC) militantly supported by bodies like the South African Students' Organisation (SASO) had been successfully mobilising the black people for the national liberation struggle in a way that made the government frustrated and bitter. The masses of the people had become as politically dedicated, alert and irrepressibly active as they once were just before the African National Congress of South Africa (ANC) and the Pan-Africanist Congress of Azania (PAC) were proscribed in 1960.

The two newspapers which were proscribed were *The World* and its sister publication the *Weekend World*. They were owned by the Argus newspaper group, a white company, but were run by Africans and circulated widely among the black community. *The World* had originally concentrated on sports and entertainment and generally avoided political issues as much as possible. But when Percy Qoboza took over its editorship in 1974 the paper changed. It tried to identify with the aspirations of the African people, especially after the 1976 student-initiated upheavals. Since its reporters were black and the black community were not hostile to *The World*, they were able to go to many places where white journalists could not enter during the Soweto anti-government campaigns. *The World* and *Weekend World* were the best sources of information on those anti-government activities. The authorities began to harass the two papers but the black journalists saw it as their political and professional duty to communicate to the public the facts of the situation as they saw them irrespective of Government feelings.

Several times the Minister of Justice, Mr J. Kruger, threatened to close the two papers, accusing them of carrying anti-government and inflamatory reports. The police even arrested individual journalists on the staff of the two papers, including Percy Qobozo himself who, in a pre-dawn raid, was taken by the police for eight hours of questioning and warned that he would be detained and his paper banned, if it continued to carry reports on exactly what black people felt and wanted in opposition to government policies.

Then came the controversial death of Steve Biko in prison on September 12, 1977, the outcry over which culminated in the banning of the 18 organisations, the two newspapers and the nation-wide arrests and restrictions. *The World* continued to publish reports on the mass meetings, protests and memorial services which were held throughout the country following the death of Biko. The people demanded an inquiry into the circumstances of Biko's death. Many white people attended these activities and protests and the white press also published material about the circumstances and controversies surrounding the death of Biko, to the complete fury and embarrassment of the government.

The 30 years old Steve Biko was a founding member and leading figure of the Black Consciousness Movement. He was a well known and highly respected leader of his people. Internationally he was respected, admired and considered a non-violent, moderate and intelligent leader by many top government officials in the western world. But because of the suppression of certain types of views in South Africa, very few whites knew who Biko was until after his controversial death which sparked off the almost incredible nation-wide anti-government activities.

According the the South African government figures and explanation, Biko was the twentieth prisoner to die in 18 months — and only five of these died of natural causes. The rest, including Biko, were said to have died as a result of self-inflicted suffocation, hanging, bleeding or starvation. Others were alleged to have died after being shot during a disturbance or attempting to run away. Those who know the South African prison conditions well were certain that most of the deaths of political prisoners were cold-blooded murder. In addition to this, Mr Jimmy Kruger said that Biko had died after only eight days of a hunger strike! Most people could not believe his explanation. Some evidence to the effect that Biko died of multiple brain and body injuries was first revealed by the press and the inconsistencies of the government version of the story continuously exposed, especially by *The World* and the *East London Daily Dispatch*, whose Editor Donald Woods was a friend and great admirer of Steve Biko.

The *East London Daily Dispatch*, traditionally a conservative, white owned and run influential daily, but read by more blacks than whites, printed on the front page of its issue of September 14, 1977 the following headline: "We salute a hero of the nation", with an editorial titled "Death of a Martyr". Donald Woods, a white liberal, did much to challenge and expose Mr Kruger's inconsistent version of the circumstances in which Biko died. Mr Woods therefore gave a lot of credibility to the interpretation that Steve Biko was murdered by the South African police.

The Afrikaans newspaper, *Die Transvaler*, said: "the death of any detainee and particularly such a symbolic figure as Biko, is political dynamite both here and abroad". The newspaper also joined those who were demanding an investigation into the death of Biko. The *Johannesburg Sunday Times* stated: "The death of Steve Biko in detention was bad enough without the squalid efforts now being made to convict him posthumously on charges that were never brought against him when he was alive to answer them".

In one of its editorials which offended the government, *The World* stated: "We intend to see to it that the truth is told about how Biko met his death and if somebody is found criminally responsible for that death, then we intend to see to it that he is nailed for it".

From their own investigations, the *Johannesburg Star* and the *Rand Daily Mail* categorically stated that Biko suffered extensive brain damage and severe bruising. The *Mail* argued that "There is one very good reason why Mr Kruger did not challenge these facts . . . Because they are true. We know they are true and we know Mr Kruger knows they are true."

Mr J. Kruger desperately tried to sue the newspapers which published information conflicting with the government's version and lodged complaints with the Press Council, a government-dominated institution, against the recalcitrant papers. When all this proved to be of no avail, the government resorted to the bannings and arrests of October 19, 1977.

The reaction of the USA and the EEC countries was significant. They began to re-examine their relations with South Africa. The US Government called on the South African Government to set up an inquiry into the death of Biko. Mr Cyrus Vance, US Secretary of State, said that he was shocked and saddened over the death of Steve Biko and that he "must be regarded as another victim of the apartheid system and the South African security legislation which supports that system".

Andrew Young, US Ambassador to the UN, compared the death of Biko, to that of President John F. Kennedy, Dr

Martin Luther King and Senator Robert Kennedy. The British Government through its Ambassador in South Africa, Sir David Scott, expressed "profound shock" and said his death would do harm to the forces favouring a non-violent solution to the problems of South Africa.

Biko's death so outraged the black people of South Africa that a torrent of anti-government activities ensued, which led to the banning of the 18 organisations and the two newspapers, accompanied by mass arrests. In turn this suppression of the opponents of apartheid led to increased international pressure against South Africa.

The nature of the repressive measures taken by the South African government clearly embarrassed its allies internationally and provoked the UN Security Council to unanimously vote to impose mandatory sanctions on the supply of arms to South Africa on November 4, 1977. South Africa was on a collision course not only with the majority of its citizens but also with the outside world. In its desperate attempt to convince the world that its internal and external enemies would not succeed in destroying the apartheid system, South Africa decided to hold a premature general election on November 30. The aim of the election was to prove that the whites were united and prepared to fight to the last ditch for their "right" to rule and oppress the black majority!

The western press for the first time agreed with what the Africans of South Africa had been saying for decades — that there is no press freedom in South Africa as understood in the West. Even the white press had little freedom not worth speaking of and that little freedom was being taken away. But since there is always a limit to how far the media, like any social institution or people, can be suppressed, the establishment media can prove useful on occasion to the liberation movement, as was demonstrated by the *East London Daily Dispatch*.

Employing the same staff and using the same printing plant, but with a white editor, Mr John Miskelly, the Argus group launched the *Post* in less than two weeks after the banning of its predecessor, *The World*. *The Post*, which is aimed at the same audience and advertisers as *The World*, is devoted to sport and entertainment. It underplays politics and reports very little of the continuing political struggles in South Africa, just as *The World* did before Percy Qobozo took over the editorship. The first issue did not even carry an editorial. Its weekend version is very similar to the banned *Weekend World* in its format. It is inevitable that some of the journalists will try to identify with the aspirations and plight of their community. They will go on articulating and communicating black anger and the progress of the resistance movement and exposing the system.

Like others before him, Donald Woods of the *East London Daily Dispatch* under house arrest is forbidden to write articles, cannot be quoted in the press, nor can he legally enter any black, coloured or Indian area, any school or university, and can talk to only one person at a time — with the exception of his family. His freedom to pursue his journalistic career was taken away. But his situation is not as bad as that of many black journalists under restriction. He continues to get his salary from his paper. He has a swimming pool, a huge back garden and a large house in which to occupy himself.

As explained elsewhere in the book, individuals, organisations and newspapers may come and go, but the liberation struggle itself continues unabated. It continuously throws up new organisations, leaders, newspapers and institutions. In spite of government's suppressive actions, the intensity of the struggle in South Africa continues to increase, producing desperation, confusion and cracks in the estbalishment edifice until the system itself collapses.

It is important to note that the difference between the situation in 1960 when liberation movements were banned and the 1977 bannings is that the liberationists in South Africa in 1977 had become more sophisticated and experienced and had benefited greatly from their past experiences. The other difference was that by 1977, the struggle for national liberation in South Africa had become accepted by the overwhelming majority of the UN members, including the major western powers, as legitimate and just. South Africa had become more isolated internationally than ever before and its policies were found indefensible even by many of the countries which were once its fervent supporters. The doctrine of "no interference in the affairs of a sovereign state" generally no longer applied to South Africa as far as the international community was concerned. What the Africans of South Africa and their allies had said decades ago, and which was then ignored if not opposed, was now recognised as fact internationally.

The reasons for this internationally favourable situation *vis a vis* the black struggle in South Africa were not far to seek. The main ones were: the continued determination, heightened struggles and selfless patriotic sacrifices of the people inside South Africa opposed to the existing system; the successful international publicity and information work, and tireless lobbying by the ANC, PAC, the Unity Movement of South Africa (UMSA) and the OAU, supported by the efforts of the socialist countries and forces, solidarity movements and people concerned with human emancipation in the West; and the victories of similar movements in the Third World. The favourability of the international situation also meant more material and moral support, which is an important element for the South African liberation fighters.

It is clear that the developments of 1977 in South Africa support the following conclusions which the reader will find in this book:

1. That there is no press freedom in South Africa worth lauding and cannot possibly be under such a repressive minortiy racist regime.
2. That in spite of the repressive nature of the political set-up in South Africa, the media continue to retain their dual nature, the *eufunctional* and *dysfunctional* aspects. The latter remains an important aspect to the liberationists and

the whole opposition movement in South Africa.
3. That the more threatened a system is, the more repressive it becomes. The more threatened and repressive it becomes, the more it suppresses people who may not necessarily be fundamentally opposed to it. The more of its own establishment people it alienates and oppresses, the quicker the system will crumble.
4. That because of attempts by the regime to maintain a democratic way of life for the whole community alone in South Africa, the establishment media remain a leading barometer of the levels of the internal contradictions within that community — contradictions which ultimately are important to those who seek to destroy that system.

C.C. Chimutengwende
November 1977

FURTHER READING

While publications of the *Centre Against Apartheid* of the UN are probably one of the best sources of information on South Africa, the following are some of the equally important sources relevant to the subject and which do not appear in the *Notes and References* at the end of each chapter of this study, but were consulted by the researcher.

Heribert, Adam (ed): *South Africa: Sociological Perspectives,* Oxford University Press, London, 1971.

Bunting, Brian: *The Rise of the South African Reich,* Penguin African Library, London, 1964.

Hodgkin, Thomas: *Nationalism in Colonial Africa,* Frederick Muller, London, 1956.

Patterson, Sheila: *A Study of the Boer People and the African Nation,* Routledge & Kegan Paul, London, 1956.

Munger, Edwin S.: *Afrikaner and African Nationalism: Parallels and Parameters,* Oxford University Press, London, 1967.

Kruger, D.W. (ed): *South African Parties and Politics,* 1910-1960, Human & Rousseau, Cape Town, 1960.

Marais, J.S.: *The Fall of Kruger's Republic,* Oxford, Clarendon Press, 1961.

Hahlo, H.R. and Kahn, E.: *The Union of South Africa: the Development of Its Laws and Constitution,* Stevens, London, 1960.

Kahn, Ellison: *The New Constitution,* Juta, Johannesburg, 1962.

Jaarsveld, F.A. van: *The Afrikaner's Interpretation of South African History,* Simondium, Cape Town, 1961.

Vatcher, W.H.: *White Laager: the Rise of Afrikaner Nationalism,* Pall Mall, London, 1965.

Simons, H.J.: *Class and Colour in South Africa, 1850-1950,* Penguin, London, 1969.

Roberts, M. and Trollip, A.: *The South African Opposition, 1939-1945,* Longmans Green, London, 1947.

Trapido, Stanley: "Political Institutions and Afrikaner Social Structures in the Republic of South Africa", in the *American Political Science Review,* March, 1963.

Randall, Peter (Ed): *Anatomy of Apartheid,* Spro-Cas, Occasional Publications No 1, Johannesburg, 1970.

Biko, B.S. (ed): *Black Viewpoint,* Spro-Cas Black Community Programmes, Durban, 1972.

Gibson, Richard: *African Liberation Movements: Contemporary Struggles Against White Minority Rule,* Oxford University Press, London.

Lewin, Julius: *Politics and Law in South Africa,* Merlin Press, London, 1963.

International Commission of Jurists: *South Africa and the Rule of Law,* Geneva, 1967.

International Commission of Jurists: *Erosion of the Rule of Law in South Africa,* Geneva, 1968.

Stuart, Kesley William and Klopper, Weston: *The Newspaperman's Guide to the Law,* Mainpress Books, Cape Town, 1968.

Blackwell, L. and Bamford, B.: *Newspaper Law of South Africa*, Juta, Cape Town, 1963.

Cutten, Theo E.: *A History of the Press in South Africa*, The National Union of South African Students, Johannesburg, 1936.

Broughton, Morris: *Press and Politics of South Africa*, Purnell, Cape Town, 1961.

Clay, George and Uys, Stanley: "The Press Strijdom's Last Barrier", in *Africa South*. October-December, 1957.

Friedgut, A.J.: "The Non-European Press" in Hellman, Ellen (ed): *Handbook on Race Relations in South Africa*, Oxford University Press, London, 1949.

Report of the Commission of Inquiry in Regard to Undesirable Publications, Government Printers, Pretoria, 1957.

Report of the Commission of Inquiry into the Press, Government Printers, Pretoria, 1962, 1964.

Smith, H. Lindsay: *Behind the Press in South Africa*, Stewart, Cape Town, 1947.

Kotze, D.A.: *African Politics in South Africa, 1964-1974*, C. Hurst, London, 1975.

Kuper, Leo: *An African Bourgeoisie: Race, Class and Politics in South Africa*, Yale University Press, New Haven, 1965.

Braverman, R.E.: "African Workers Advance", in the *African Communist*, London, 1973.

Lee, Branc: "Strikes in South Africa", *Review of International Affairs*, Belgrade, 1973.

Malapo, N. and Ngotyana: "African Workers and the National Struggle", in the *African Communist*, London, 1971.

Teplinskie, L.B.: *Hotbed of Racialism and Neo-colonialism*, Novosti Press Agency Publishing House, Moscow, 1972.

Horwitz, Rolf: "South Africa: the Background to Sanctions", in *Political Quarterly*, London, April-June, 1971.

Essack, A.K., "Vorster Offers Bogus Independence", in the *Review of International Affairs*, Belgrade, 1971.

Heribert, Adam: "The South African Power-Elite: a Survey of Ideological Commitment", *Canadian Journal of Political Science*, Toronto, March 1971.

Buthelezi, Gatsha: "My Role Within Separate Development Politics", *Sechaba*, ANC, London, March 1973.

Hugo, P.J.: "Separate Development: outside criticism and South Africa's reaction thereto", in the *Journal of Racial Affairs*, Pretoria, October, 1969.

Duru, Julius, O.: "The Dilemma of Foreign Investment in South Africa", in *Proceedings of the American Society of International Law* at its 65th Meeting, 1971, Washington, DC, 1971.

Hepple, Alex: *South African Workers Under Apartheid*, London, Christian Action Publications, 1969, International Defence and Aid Fund for Southern Africa.

deKlerk, W.: *The Puritans' South Africa*, Rex Collings, London, 1975.

Johnson, R.W.: *How Will South Africa Survive*, MacMillan, London, 1977.

INDEX

192